The Secrets of Tutankhamen

Leonard Cottrell

Evans Brothers Limited
Two Continents

Contents

The author and publishers are indebted to Cassell and Co Ltd for permission to quote from *The Tomb of Tut-ankh-amen* by Howard Carter and A. C. Mace.

Most of the photographs in this book were taken at the time of the discovery of the tomb and are reproduced by permission of the Griffith Institute, Oxford.

For permission to reproduce other photographs the author and publishers are indebted to Lehnert and Landrock for Akhenaten, Nefertiti and Queen Tiye; BOAC for the Temple of Queen Hatshepsut; the British Museum for Amun-Re and the cuneiform writing; and Rex Keating for the illustration of the final stage of stripping a mummy.

To all young people who want to be
archaeologists

The Secrets of
Tutankhamen

Introduction

When Howard Carter discovered the tomb of King Tutankhamen in 1922, he revealed to the modern world an unprecedented sight—the virtually undisturbed magnificence of an Egyptian royal burial. To the excavation-weary Carter and his loyal crew, the find was a miraculous culmination of what had seemed an almost hopeless quest.

Carter and his team had been digging in Egypt's Valley of the Kings for years without success. The Valley lies just a few miles from the west bank of the Nile, opposite Karnak and Luxor and more than four hundred miles south of present-day Cairo. It had been the royal necropolis of Thebes, the ancient capital of the Egyptian empire at the zenith of its power.

With the end of the reign of the pharaohs, Thebes passed successively through the hands of the Persians, the Greeks of Alexander the Great, the Romans, the Arabs, and the Ottoman Empire. In modern times Egypt was invaded by Napoleon; later the country became a British protectorate with its own ruling house.

For hundreds of years, the Valley and its surrounding desert, wild and inaccessible, had been the haunt of bandits. Only in the 19th century, as a measure of order was imposed, did archaeologists dare to begin excavating there.

In all, about thirty-three royal tombs had been uncovered in the bedrock of the Valley or dug into its furrowed rock walls, but every one had been pillaged long before by

Detail of King Tutankhamen's Kherp *sceptre—symbol of authority used in connection with offerings.*

professional thieves, some only a few years after their occupants were buried. The Europeans had found only some scattered objects left behind by the robbers. Few important discoveries had been made in the Valley since the start of the twentieth century; most experts believed that the burial ground had yielded all its secrets.

Carter hoped for more. Financed by his sponsor, the Earl of Carnarvon, he had searched fruitlessly for fifteen years. In 1922, Lord Carnarvon informed Carter that he had decided not to apply for a renewal of his government concession to excavate in the Valley. He had spent 20,000 pounds—well over $500,000 in today's dollars—and had nothing to show for it but holes in the sand.

Carter pleaded for one more season. He was convinced that one small triangle in the Valley that he had not yet examined was n ore than likely the site of Tutankhamen's tomb. Carnarvon was not enthusiastic, but when Carter offered to pay for the dig himself if it should prove unsuccessful, his patron reluctantly agreed.

Had Carter not persisted so stubbornly, who knows how much longer it would have been before these astonishing treasures were brought to light? It is certainly possible that our generation would never have seen them. But on November 26, 1922, in the presence of a hastily-summoned Lord Carnarvon, Carter drilled a small hole in a sealed door his workers had uncovered. Almost speechless, he had his first indication of the incalculable riches of history and art that lay within.

Carter refused to begin clearing the tomb until he had engaged a team of experts to assist him. Among these was the photographer Harry Burton, of New York's Metropolitan Museum of Art. Burton was to photograph every stage of the six-year excavation. It is his photographs, in large part, that accompany Leonard Cottrell's knowledgeable account in the pages of this book.

As Cottrell shows, the discovery of the tomb was hardly the whole story. The delicate task of excavating the tomb without destroying its 3,000-year-old contents, the quarrels, the sensational publicity, even a legend of a "curse" on the man who opened the tomb—all of these were the heavy price the young archaeologist had to pay for his discovery. But, resisting reporters, ignoring hampering sightseers and conflicting government claims, Carter pressed on, carefully and with commendable restraint. In this book, and in the dazzling exhibition produced by the Metropolitan Museum of Art in 1976, we see the result.

Sponsors of "The Treasures of Tutankhamun" used Carter's original check list of the excavation and Burton's photographs to guide them in mounting the show, which was sent on a three-year tour of the United States to be seen by millions. The show's fifty-five breathtaking artifacts were arranged in approximately the same order as they had originally been excavated. The Tutankhamen treasures, which are owned by the Egyptian government, were borrowed for this unique exhibit under a special agreement made by U.S. Secretary of State Henry Kissinger and the Egyptian Foreign Minister. Proceeds of the show were earmarked for the renovation of the Cairo Museum and the permanent reinstallation of the Tutankhamen treasures there.

Leonard Cottrell, the author of THE SECRETS OF TUTANKHAMEN and many other books on Egyptology was, by his own admission, an amateur in the field of archaeology. He was, however, an amateur with years of devoted research and writing to his credit. He explained his interest in Egyptology by quoting a "real" Egyptologist, Arthur Weigall:

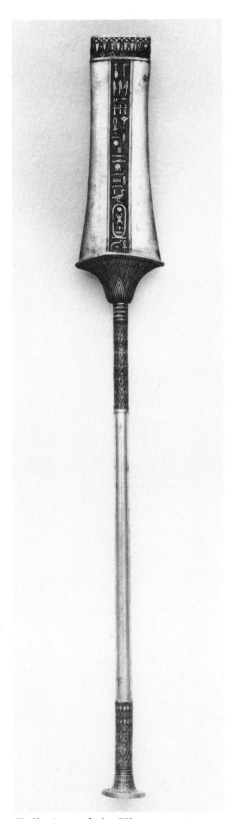

Full view of the Kherp *sceptre.*

Bezel of scarab depicting the King between the god Atum (left) and the sun-god Horus (right), the latter deity giving Tutankhamen the symbol of life. Above the King is the solar disc radiating life and below is a decorative device symbolizing the 'Union of the Two Kingdoms', Upper and Lower Egypt.

"A man has no more right to think of the people of old as dust than he has to think of his contemporaries as lumps of meat. The true archaeologist does not take pleasure in skeletons, for his whole effort is to cover them decently with flesh and skin once more, and to put some thoughts back in the empty skulls. Nor does he delight in ruined buildings because they are ruined . . . He is such an enemy of Death and Decay that he would rob them of their harvest; and for every life that the foe has claimed he would raise up, if he could, a memory that would continue to live."

The Secrets of
Tutankhamen

1 The Valley of the Kings

Near the little town of Luxor, some six hundred miles up the river Nile, in Upper Egypt, lies a lonely valley. The rocky hills which surround it are not very high, though their dramatic shapes, stark against the blue sky, make them look bigger than they are. There is no river running through the valley; there are no trees or bushes, not even a flower. The landscape is as barren as a crater on the moon. Such beauty as it possesses comes mainly from the quality of its colour and the varying light which plays upon it. At midday in summer the towering cliffs fling back a fierce glare which makes the traveller half close his eyes. In early morning and late afternoon the valley is pure gold, except in the shadowed clefts where the colours range from russet to deep purple.

At the highest point rises a mountain shaped like a pyramid, which at dawn catches the morning sun while the rest of the valley is still in shadow. To the Ancient Egyptians this was the home of a goddess, Merit-Segert, the 'Lover of Silence'. An ancient saying reads 'Beware the Goddess of the Western Peak . . . she strikes instantly and without warning.' But when you look more closely at the valley you notice something unusual. At intervals along the steep cliffs, or among mounds of sand and rock lower down, are gaping holes; some are small apertures, others have monumental gateways leading to shafts cut into the hillside. These are the entrances to tombs which were made between three thousand five hundred and three thousand years ago, a period during which the Pharaohs, or kings, of Ancient Egypt ruled over a great empire and enjoyed enormous wealth. Each one,

This statuette, which is mounted on a gold and silver ceremonial stick, represents Tutankhamen at about 12 years of age when he ascended the throne

7

The royal cemetery with its guardian peak above

when he died, was buried in a magnificent tomb hollowed out of the mountain. Some of these sepulchres were hundreds of feet deep; long galleries were hewn out of the rock leading to chamber after chamber until at last they opened on to the 'Golden Hall', where the body of the Pharaoh lay in the full panoply of his greatness, enclosed in a golden coffin which, in turn, nested within other larger coffins, elaborately inlaid with semi-precious stones.

Around these coffins was built a series of wooden structures, like huge boxes, also plated with thick gold. And in adjoining rock-cut rooms were all the things which the Pharaoh would want in the after life: his rich furniture, beds, chairs, tables, chests, his royal chariots for

8

hunting and warfare; his weapons, clothing, even games—one of them rather like chess—with which to while away his leisure time. And, of course, an abundance of food and wine. For the Ancient Egyptians believed that their kings and other great ones would need, in the after life, all the possessions which had made their lives enjoyable on earth. Not only that; they believed the soul, or *ka* (as they called it) of the dead Pharaoh could not survive to enjoy life beyond the grave unless his earthly body was preserved against violation and decay. That was why they buried the royal bodies in these deep, elaborate tombs, and why they went to such trouble and expense to embalm them, and protect them from robbers.

Yet they failed.

Despite all these precautions—the deep shafts, concealed entrances, 'puzzle-passages', blind alleys designed to fool robbers; despite the ponderous stone sarcophagi weighing many tons, and the lonely remoteness of the Royal Valley itself, with its watchful priests and guardian soldiers, the robbers got through. When the kingdom was strong and the Valley well guarded, the dead Pharaohs were reasonably secure. But there came times when weak rulers and corrupt officials gave the cunning and determined tomb robbers their chance. How they did it we do not know, but most probably they bribed the guards and then tunnelled, at night, through tons of rubble filling the passages until they reached the burial chamber and its rich contents. In doing this the plunderers showed great courage. Not only were they risking being caught, but they were violating the sepulchre of a deity, for to them the dead Pharaoh was a god. Yet they did it, not once but repeatedly. We know this because, by a lucky chance, actual documents have survived, dating from before 1000 B.C., setting down the evidence given by the tomb-robbing gangs when they were brought for trial. Here is a statement by one of the robbers, Amenpnufer:

'We went to rob the tombs in accordance with

A pair of the king's ear-rings

9

our regular habit, and we found the pyramid of Sekhemre-shedtaui, the son of Re, Sebekemsaf, this not being at all like the pyramids and tombs of the nobles which we habitually went to rob . . . When we broke through the rubble . . . we found this God lying at the back of his burial place. And we found the burial place of Nubkhaas, his queen, situated beside him. . . . We opened their sarcophagi and their coffins in which they were, and found the noble mummy of this King equipped with a falchion [a type of sword]. . . . The noble mummy of this King was completely bedecked with gold, and his coffins were adorned with gold and silver inside and out. . . . We collected the gold we found on the noble mummy of this God . . . and we collected all that we found on her likewise; and we set fire to their coffins. We took their furniture, articles of gold, silver and bronze, and divided them among ourselves.'

The sepulchre of Sebekemsaf was that of a relatively minor king, so one may imagine how such mighty rulers as Seti I, Ramesses II and others were equipped.

Robberies like this were so frequent that a time came when the priests responsible for guarding the Royal Valley despaired of protecting the bodies of the Pharaohs in their original tombs. So they hit on a desperate and ingenious plan. One night—it must have been at night to avoid detection—they secretly gathered together some thirty royal and princely mummies, took them from their own tombs, carried them up a steep mountain track and lowered them, one by one, into a deep rock-cut shaft on the eastern side of the Theban cliffs—facing the Nile.

At the foot of this deep hole a horizontal shaft ran for some distance into the rock, ending in a chamber. Within this chamber the royal bodies—some of which had been rewrapped several times—were placed in orderly rows. To most of them the priests attached little labels inscribed with the name of the king, queen, or prince, sometimes stating how many times the body had been removed. These priestly officials were orderly and systematic. It must have

A richly decorated ceremonial baton

10

annoyed them greatly to have seen the royal tombs robbed again and again, the bodies unceremoniously tumbled out of their coffins, the mummy wrappings stripped, the furniture stolen, and the priests left to tidy up the mess. So they were careful to attach to each of the bodies a neatly written label giving its history.

We have no written record of this operation, but in 1881 an archaeologist named Emil Brughsch came upon the secret burial place at Deir el Bahari, to which he had been guided by Arab tomb-robbers who had already discovered and partially plundered it. In fact they would have stolen all the bodies but for the fact that it would have been impossible to conceal the operation from the eyes of the Egyptian Department of Antiquities. Thus the priests' three-thousand-year-old secret was revealed at last; their ruse had, most astonishingly, been successful, and the Pharaohs had slept in peace for thirty centuries.

Among the royal bodies found in the cache were some of the greatest Pharaohs of Ancient Egypt: such men as Seti I, Ramesses II, Amenophis I, Tuthmosis I, II and III. In all, as Brughsch wrote at that time: there were 'thirty-six coffins, all belonging to Kings or Queens or Princesses.' Only one was found in his original tomb, and that was Amenophis II. Some years later, a French archaeologist named Loret discovered the tomb of this great monarch in the Royal Valley. It had, of course, been robbed in ancient times; little furniture was left, but the tomb had been utilized by the priests as a second repository for royal bodies. There lay Amenophis II, the warrior king, in his original sarcophagus, and beside him rested the great bow which, according to an inscription, he had boasted that only he could draw. With him were twelve more royal bodies, including Merenptah, thought by some scholars to have been the Pharaoh of the Exodus who was drowned in the Red Sea. But there he was, together with Tuthmosis IV and his son Amenophis III, the father of the famous 'Heretic King' Akhenaten.

At the base of the rock-cleft on the right is the secret shaft in which the bodies of over thirty kings lay undiscovered for 3,000 years

11

Stripping a mummy—the last stage

At first it was decided to let Amenophis II rest in his original tomb, together with his bow and a beautiful funerary boat. But not for long. The modern successors of the ancient Egyptian tomb robbers would not leave the tomb alone. The Chief Inspector at Luxor—the man responsible for guarding and protecting the antiquities—was a young Englishman named Howard Carter. When he entered the newly plundered tomb of Amenophis II, he found that the body had been stripped and tossed on to the floor, and what remained of the funerary furniture had been stolen. The guards told him that they had been overpowered by armed robbers.

Carter wrote at the time: 'The bandages had been ripped open, but the body not broken. This had evidently been done by an expert, as only the pieces where objects are usually found had been touched. The boat in the antechamber had been stolen, the mummy that was upon it was lying on the floor and had been smashed to pieces. I carefully examined the wrappings of the royal mummy to see if there were any signs of their having contained jewellery, but could find no trace.'

In fact, the ancient Egyptian tomb robbers, who had plundered the same sepulchre some three thousand years earlier, had left nothing for their modern successors to find.

Discoveries such as this, made toward the end of the last century, inspired other explorers to dig in the Valley. Admittedly most of the great tombs had been robbed—indeed, more than twenty of them had been tourist attractions as far back as Greek and Roman times, between two thousand five hundred and two thousand years ago. Greek and Roman tourists used to inscribe their initials on the walls, where they can still be seen, while the smoke of their torches has blackened the roofs of the empty sepulchres. Yet there existed lists of Pharaohs, kept by the priests, and in these lists were names of one or two kings not yet accounted for. Perhaps there was a faint chance that one or two of these tombs had been overlooked by the robbers?

12

So archaeologists, professional and amateur, came to the Valley, dug and redug, combing the barren cliffs from end to end, excavating hundreds of tons of rock and sand, but with sparse results. Loret was the most fortunate discoverer. After him came an American named Theodore Davis who, in 1903, came upon the tomb of two Theban nobles, Prince Yuya and his wife Thuya, a find which yielded specimens of chariots and other funerary furniture—the best-preserved examples found up to that date. Four years later Davis, assisted by an archaeologist named Ayrton, found another small rock-cut tomb containing a large gilded wooden shrine, much damaged, with a damaged coffin containing the body of a young man. The tomb was dated toward the end of the Eighteenth Dynasty (1555–1350 B.C.); the gilded shrine was inscribed with the name of Queen Tiye—wife of Amenophis III and mother of Akhenaten; but no one has yet decided to whom the coffin belonged, or the name of the young man inside it.

Queen Tiye, the mother of Akhenaten

That appeared to be the end of the great discoveries. Davis went on digging, year after year, but without result. In 1914, at the outbreak of the First World War, he relinquished the concession granted to him by the Egyptian Government and stated candidly that, in his opinion, no more royal tombs would ever be found. The Royal Valley had been exhausted.

2 The Discoverers

The handle of a ceremonial walking-stick covered with thin gold foil. The head, arms and feet of the African prisoner represented are of ebony and exquisitely carved

When young Howard Carter came to Egypt for the first time he was eighteen. Normally he could never have afforded the cost of the trip from England, for his father was a struggling artist who made his living painting portraits of animals. This may seem a strange pursuit, but in those days—some seventy years ago—gentlemen, fond of riding and hunting, used to commission painters to make portraits of their favourite horses. Young Howard seems to have inherited his father's talent, and after leaving school he obtained part-time work copying pictures and inscriptions brought back from Egypt by Egyptologists. One of these scholars, the late Professor Newberry, admired Carter's gifts so much that he arranged to pay his fare and expenses to Egypt so that he could copy certain paintings in the tombs at Beni Hasan.

Howard, a very bright London boy, fell in love with Egypt, as many have done before and since his time. He had a good ear for languages, soon learned sufficient Arabic to get by, and plunged himself wholeheartedly into the exciting world of Egyptology. He had the advantage of working with scholars, but he also read deeply and widely, to such good effect that in time he obtained a minor post in the Department of Antiquities of the Egyptian Government, the department which is responsible for protecting the antiquities of the Nile Valley and sometimes conducts excavations.

But Howard Carter had another greater advantage. He was good with his hands; he had an extraordinary practical skill in excavating and preserving frail objects of antiquity. Also he knew the peasants of Upper Egypt, where he

14

was stationed. These men, many of whom lived on the site of the ancient tombs, had for generations made a skilled profession of tomb-robbery, and 'illicit digging'. Into the constant battle of wits between them and the Department of Antiquities, Carter entered with zest. In his job he had to be not only an archaeologist, but also a policeman and detective. For instance, when the tomb of Amenophis II was robbed, the guards stated that they had been overcome by armed intruders. But Carter was suspicious. Inspecting the padlock, he found it had been 'fixed' with silver paper so that it appeared to be locked though it was not. Later he traced the actual robber by the imprint of his sandals on the dusty floor of the tomb. The man belonged to the family of Abderassul, the same family which had discovered the famous burial cache of the Pharaohs at Deir el Bahari.

On another occasion, having had wind of the fact that certain men were going to make an attack on the tomb of Queen Hatshepsut, high up in the Theban cliffs, Carter and his guards laid in wait for them at night, and in the brisk gun battle which ensued the robbers were driven off. Carter did his job well; he instituted a system of reliable guardians, called *ghaffirs;* he protected the principal tombs with iron gates, and took other precautions which at least minimized illegal digging for antiquities and the defacing of tomb sepulchres. For by this time—the beginning of this century—interest in Ancient Egypt had reached a point at which art dealers were prepared to pay high prices for a piece of sculpture hacked from the wall of a tomb, and the genial desperados of El Gournah (the Arab village built in the ancient cemetery) were always ready to supply this demand. They even sunk holes in the floors of their huts and built passages leading to the tombs!

Eventually Carter was appointed Chief Inspector of the Theban Necropolis—a splendid-sounding title which is still held by the modern occupant of the position. This official is responsible for guarding and preserving the richest and most important archaeological site in Egypt,

The funerary temple of Queen Hatshepsut at Deir el Bahari

15

which includes not only the Valley of the Kings but the numerous tombs of the nobles and high officers of Pharaoh built in the cliffs facing the Nile. The Chief Inspector also carried out important excavations. Sometimes there were wealthy foreign amateurs who enjoyed wintering in Luxor, and who became interested in Egyptology and were prepared to finance excavations. Among these was Theodore Davis, who had worked on the tomb of Yuya and Thuya in 1903 but after twelve years' excavation had decided that the Royal Valley had been combed clean. When he relinquished the concession granted to him by the Egyptian Government, it was taken up by a new amateur archaeologist, Lord Carnarvon. Since the Egyptian authorities took care that actual archaeological work was

Head-rest carved of ivory

supervised by professionals, Howard Carter was 'assigned' to Lord Carnarvon.

There could hardly be a greater contrast than that between Carter and Carnarvon—between the almost self-taught professional archaeologist and the English aristocrat to whom Egyptology was a hobby. Apart from his salary Carter had no money; Carnarvon was a man of high birth and considerable wealth. And excavation—even in those days—was an expensive business. It had to be carried out systematically over a period of years, and beside the wages of the numerous workmen there would often be the salaries of specialists called in if an important discovery was made. Carnarvon financed the excavation of the Royal Valley, and of course took a close interest in it. But it was Carter who, from his long experience, selected the sites to be dug, and supervised the work. Excavation was normally carried out only from autumn to early spring; in summer the weather became too hot.

Owing to the outbreak of the First World War, not much excavation was carried out until 1917, but from then onwards, for five years, Carter and Carnarvon patiently explored, moving hundreds of tons of sand and rubble left by previous investigators, redigging sites which had already been dug on the off-chance that a tomb entrance had been overlooked in that tumbled wilderness of sand and rock chippings. It seemed a forlorn hope, but they went on, year after year, even though Sir Gaston Maspero, the Director of the Antiquities Department, agreed with Davis that the Valley had been exhausted.

Eventually, by the end of the 1921 season, Carnarvon decided to give up. During the summer of 1922, when both men were back in England, Lord Carnarvon invited Carter to his country home, Highclere Castle, and informed him that, in view of the expense of excavation, and the fruitless results of their joint labours, he had decided to discontinue further excavation. Carter understood and shared his patron's disappointment, but pleaded with him to continue for one more season. There were two main reasons, he said, why he wished to do

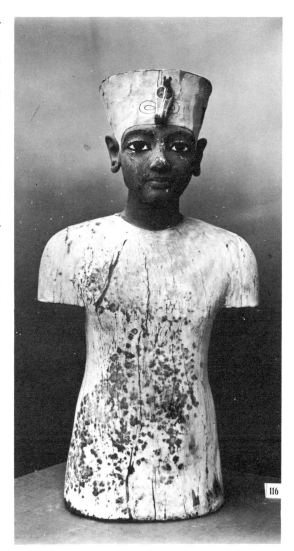

The king's mannequin of carved wood, covered with gesso and painted. It was probably used for the king's jewellery or robes

17

The entrance to the tomb as first seen by Carter and his workmen

this. First, in the previous year, 1921, he had come upon a small, shallow pit containing a few scraps of fabric and some jar sealings bearing the name of Tutankhamen, a Pharaoh whose tomb had never been found. He was not an important king and had reigned for only a few years. Still he was a Pharaoh; his name was on the 'King-lists' kept by the ancient priests, and the presence of these scraps of fabric and jar sealings, which might have been connected with a funeral ceremony, suggested to Carter that the tomb might be found nearby. Carnarvon was sceptical.

Carter then produced the well-worn map of the Royal Valley which they had used for so many seasons. They had worked systematically, combing the Valley foot by foot, and as each area had been cleared and nothing found, that area was marked off on the map. But, Carter pointed out, there was still one small triangular area, covered with sand and rock chippings, which had not been cleared, partly because it was immediately in front of the well-known empty tomb of Ramesses VI which was frequently visited by tourists. Twice before Carter had proposed digging in this area but had stopped. On the first occasion he had been working for Theodore Davis, who had suggested that he shift to a more favourable spot. On the second he had decided to reserve clearance for a time when there would be no interference from visitors. Carter declared that once he had satisfied himself that the twice-overlooked site concealed nothing, he too would be convinced that further work was futile. Would Carnarvon please finance one more season's excavation?

To Carter's intense relief his patron agreed, and the two men parted, Carter to return to Egypt, while Carnarvon stayed in England until he was ready to join his colleague.

On October 28, 1922, Carter was back in the little town of Luxor, re-enrolling his workmen for what he believed would be his last season's excavation for Carnarvon. On November 1 he was back in the mysterious Valley. There lay the great mounds of chippings left by previous

18

excavators, and there, like black mouths in the cliffs, gaped the entrances to the plundered tombs of thirty Pharaohs, seeming to mock the efforts of the archaeologist. Carter and his men began systematically to clear the area in front of the tomb of Ramesses VI. What happened four days later is best described in Carter's own words:

'By late afternoon of the third, my men had laid bare the foundation stones of a row of ancient workmens' huts beneath which we had never probed. Hardly had I arrived . . . the next morning, than the unusual silence, due to the stoppage of work, made me realise that something out of ordinary had happened . . . The workmen had discovered a step cut in the rock immediately under the first hut to be attacked. It seemed almost too good to be true, but a short amount of extra clearing revealed the fact that we were actually in the entrance of a steep cut in the rock some thirteen feet below the entrance to the tomb of Ramesses VI.'

The Valley of the Tomb of the Kings. The guarded entrance to Tutankhamen's tomb

That step was the first of sixteen leading down into the rock. At the bottom was a blocked doorway. There was no plunderers' hole in the blocking as in so many similar entrances. Moreover, impressed in the plaster which covered the blocking stones were the seals of the Necropolis priests, placed there some three thousand years ago. The seals showed the familiar sign of the Royal Necropolis 'the jackal and nine captives', but Carter could find no seal indicating the tomb's owner. Nevertheless two facts were clear: the tomb must have belonged to someone of importance because of the royal seal, and the door could not have been opened since, at the latest, the time of the Twentieth Dynasty (1200-1090 B.C.) because the workmen's huts, which screened the entrance from above, were of that date.

Carter wrote: 'It was a thrilling moment. Alone, save for my native workmen, I found myself after ten years of comparatively unproductive labour on the threshold of what might prove to be a magnificent discovery. Anything, literally anything might lie beyond that passage,

19

and it needed all my self-control to keep from breaking down the doorway and investigating then and there.'

But Carter refilled the entrance stairway again, mounted a strong guard over it, and recrossed the Nile to the telegraph office. Later that day the distinguished archaeologist and philologist Sir Alan Gardiner was just sitting down to dinner at his home in England when the telephone rang. Lord Carnarvon was on the line. 'Listen to this', he said. 'I've just had a wire from Carter. It reads "At last you have made wonderful discovery in Valley; a magnificent tomb with seals intact; re-covered same for your arrival. Congratulations. Carter." '

Lord Carnarvon, accompanied by his daughter, Lady Evelyn Herbert, went out to Egypt as quickly as possible, and joined Carter at Luxor on November 23. Carnarvon had asked Sir Alan Gardiner to go with them, since if the tomb was that of the missing Pharaoh, Tutankhamen, it would probably contain inscriptions which would interest Gardiner. But Sir Alan wished to spend Christmas at home with his children and did not go out until early in the following year.

On the afternoon of November 24, the staircase having again been completely cleared, Carter found something which had been invisible before. Besides the familiar Necropolis seal of the 'jackal and nine captives' were others, and these bore the unmistakable name of Tutankhamen. This raised the excavator's hopes, but there was another, disquieting discovery. Careful examination of the doorway showed that it had been *twice* opened and resealed in ancient times, and the Necropolis seal was on the reclosed part of the door. Therefore the tomb was probably not intact, as Carter had hoped. The resealing was clear evidence that at some remote time thieves had entered it; later it had been reclosed by the priests.

The decisive moment had arrived.

'With trembling hands,' wrote Carter, 'I made a tiny breach in the upper left-hand corner.

Darkness and blank space, as far as an iron testing-rod could reach. . . . Candle tests were applied as a precaution against possible foul gases, and then, widening the hole a little, I inserted the candle and peered in, Lord Carnarvon, Lady Evelyn Herbert and Callender [Mr. A. R. Callender, one of Carter's assistants] standing anxiously beside me to hear the verdict. At first I could see nothing, the hot air escaping from the chamber causing the candle to flicker. But presently, as my eyes grew accustomed to the light, details of the room emerged slowly from the mist, strange animals, statues, and gold—everywhere the glint of gold. For a moment—an eternity it must have seemed to the others standing by, I was struck dumb; then Lord Carnarvon inquired anxiously—"Can you see anything?"

"Yes," I replied, . . . wonderful things. . . ." ' *The interior of the Antechamber*

21

3 The Pharaoh's Treasure

A wooden gold-plated statuette representing the king as the youthful warrior Horus

The news of this discovery, flashed across the world, had an impact such as no archaeological find has ever made. The press of the world sent their reporters hotfoot to Luxor; visitors packed the hotels, and suddenly Carnarvon and Carter, who had been carrying on their work quietly for five years, found themselves internationally known figures. The presence of so many visitors was embarrassing, for Carter was about to perform one of the most difficult, delicate, and responsible tasks ever entrusted to an archaeologist. He was not at the best of times an even-tempered man, and the additional strain frayed his nerves almost beyond endurance. Quarrels ensued, even between Carter and his friend and patron, Lord Carnarvon, chiefly over what should be done with the treasures which the tomb contained. Carter believed that they should go to the Department of Antiquities of the Egyptian Government. Carnarvon, who had financed the discovery, believed he had a right to retain at least some of the objects.

It is not the purpose of this book to enter into these arguments; they are only mentioned to illustrate the emotional atmosphere in which the clearing of the tomb was conducted, at least in the early days. Carter once remarked bitterly that it was like asking a surgeon to conduct a critical operation with the press of the world jogging his elbow. And the operation certainly was critical. Carter had discovered what appeared to be the only intact—or reasonably intact—tomb of a Pharaoh ever found; it was probably the only example which would ever be found. Within that outer chamber—already glimpsed by Carter—lay scores of precious, unique

22

Interior of the Antechamber—the northern end

objects, the funerary equipment of a king who had died more than three thousand years ago.

For thirty centuries they had been sealed in an airtight chamber—objects made of inlaid wood, gold, silver and semi-precious stones. How were they to be preserved intact? Would some of them disintegrate when exposed to the outer air? Could this be prevented? What were the best chemical methods to use? Above all, to Carter, as to all serious archaeologists, archaeology was a search for knowledge and not a mere treasure hunt. Therefore, whatever happened, means *must* be found of recording accurately the objects, the positions in which they were found, and, with the aid of specialists, of gleaning every bit of information this unique discovery might yield. It had to be a team job; there must be someone

23

The diadem discovered encircling the king's head. It is made of gold inlaid with carnelian and bordered with lapis-lazuli

to undertake the photography, a botanist to examine the plant specimens, a philologist to deal with the inscriptions, chemists to advise on the best way of preserving fragile objects, especially those of wool and fabric, and so on.

But Carter was the leader and inspirer of the team. Gardiner says of him: 'He had a lot to contend with—official interference, irritating delays, misunderstanding and a surfeit of unwelcome publicity, and perhaps he was not the best-tempered of men. But he was a superb draughtsman. He was nearly a genius in the practical mechanics of excavation, and in the recording and preservation of fragile objects of antiquity. But his greatest gift was patience.'

The outer, sealed door opened into the first of several chambers. Let us listen to another voice—that of the late Professor James Breastead, the famous American archaeologist, describing the scene when the blocking was completely removed and the excavators were able to enter the Antechamber—the first human beings to tread that floor since about 1400 B.C.

'We saw an incredible vision . . . an impossible scene from a fairy-tale, an enchanted property-room from an opera house of some great composer's dreams. Opposite us were three couches on which the King had lain, all about us were chests, caskets, alabaster vases, gold-embellished stools and chairs—the heaped-up riches of a Pharaoh who had died . . . before Crete had passed her zenith, before Greece had been born or Rome conceived, or more than half the history of civilization had taken place. . . . Against the white limestone wall, the colours of all these things were vibrant yet soft—a medley of brown, yellow, blue, amber, gold, russet and black.'

The Antechamber, as Carter called it, was not very large, much smaller than the chambers in most Egyptian royal sepulchres, but it was crammed with objects piled up in no sort of order. In fact Gardiner said they looked like furniture in a warehouse, tidily arranged, but without any regard for artistic grouping—except for two items, and these immediately

24

riveted the attention of the explorers. At the far end of the crowded chamber stood two life-size figures of wood, coloured black and gold, and each wearing on its forehead the golden uraeus— sign of royalty; each carried in its right hand a gold wand of office. Between these two guardian figures Carter and his colleagues saw yet another blocked doorway, also bearing the seals of the Royal Necropolis. 'Behind the sealed door there were to be other chambers, perhaps a succession of them, and in one of them beyond the shadow of doubt, we should see the Pharaoh lying.'

When the archaeologists had recovered a little from their first bewilderment and wonder, they began a systematic examination of the Ante-chamber, and soon they noticed something else. Everywhere there was evidence of a hasty tidying-up. Not all the objects were intact. Thieves must have entered and been inter-rupted before they could do much damage. To the left of the doorway, under one of the gold-encased wooden couches, was the open entrance to yet another, smaller chamber, on the floor of which still lay objects scattered in confusion by the thieves.

Yet very little of importance was missing or damaged. It was a miracle, but there could be no doubt that since that abortive raid, made some three thousand years ago, no one had entered the tomb of Tutankhamen. Alone among all the Pharaohs of Egypt's Imperial Age he had slept securely in his original sepulchre and was, in fact, still sleeping behind that blocked door guarded by the two sentinel figures.

It was here that Carter's patience showed itself. The temptation to break down that door and see what lay beyond must have been ex-tremely strong; but he resisted it, resolving first to clear the Antechamber and the small annex to it, taking every possible care to preserve the multitude of objects they contained. In order to do this he and Carnarvon gathered around them a team of experts, all of whom deserve honour for the work they did. There was Albert M. Lythgoe, then Curator of the Egyptian Department of the Metropolitan

One of the two wooden figures guarding the blocked doorway

The plunderers' hole to the Annex

Museum of Art, New York; Herbert E. Winlock and Arthur C. Mace, also from the Metropolitan Museum. Professor Percy Newberry was called in to help in identifying the wreaths and other plants found in the tomb; Sir Alan Gardiner was to examine the inscriptions, if any were found. There was Harry Burton, the photographer; Hall and Hauser, draughtsmen; and A. Lucas, Director of the Chemical Department of the Egyptian Government, who gave of his vast experience in the protection and preservation of Egyptian antiquities. The preliminary work alone, before a single object was removed, took two months.

Carter wrote: 'It was slow work, painfully slow, and nerve-racking at that, for one felt all the time a heavy weight of responsibility. Every excavator must, if he has any archaeo-

26

logical conscience at all. . . . The things he finds are not his own property to treat as he pleases. They are a strict legacy from the past to the present age, and if by carelessness, slackness or ignorance he lessens the sum of knowledge that might have been obtained from them he knows himself to be guilty of an archaeological crime.'

The largest tomb in the Royal Valley is that of Seti I, which has many spacious galleries and chambers. Carter obtained permission to have it temporarily closed to visitors so that he could use it as a laboratory and workshop. In this way each object, as it was removed from Tutankhamen's tomb, could be first taken to the laboratory for treatment before being packed for transport to Cairo, six hundred miles away. Every day huge throngs of visitors and journalists hung around the Valley, hoping to see some new object removed from the tomb to the laboratory. It was the only chance which most of the newspapermen had of seeing the objects, for reasons which will appear later, and which caused much bitterness. Carter and his colleagues worked through the long hot days, and often far into the night, in the lamplit interior of Seti's tomb. Every article was photographed, drawn, and recorded in Carter's precise handwriting on index-file cards which can still be seen at the Griffiths Institute, Oxford.

In the next chapter we shall examine some of the more wonderful of these objects, but meanwhile we must pause to describe briefly some of the difficulties which dogged Carter and his team during that first, exhausting season, and the atmosphere of frantic sensationalism which surrounded it.

One newspaper, the London *Daily Telegraph* thus described the scene on January 25, 1923: 'The scene . . . awakened memories of Derby Day. The road leading to the rock-enclosed ravine . . . was packed with vehicles and animals of every conceivable variety. The guides, donkey-boys, sellers of antiquities, and hawkers of lemonade were doing a roaring trade. . . . When the last article had been removed from the

A head of the god Bes on the first state chariot

27

Interior of the Antechamber, southern end, showing the couches and chariots

corridor today the newspaper correspondents began a spirited dash across the desert to the banks of the Nile on donkeys, horses, camels and chariot-like sand-carts in a race to be the first to reach the telegraph offices.'

This was bad enough, but the throngs of visitors made matters even worse. 'There were days,' wrote Carter, 'in which we actually had ten parties of visitors, and if we had given way to every demand there would not have been a day in which we did not exceed the ten. In other words there would have been weeks and weeks at a time when no work would have been done at all.' As a result of the archaeologists' firmness in limiting these unwelcome visits, they were accused of selfishness, bad manners, even boorishness; yet, if Carter had admitted more than a limited number of people to the tomb at a time, there was a grave danger that some of the precious things would have been damaged.

Carnarvon, in his turn, was attacked in the

28

press for having made *The Times* his sole agent for the distribution of news. Naturally the other newspapers were furious. One correspondent wrote of Carnarvon: ' . . . the tomb is not his private property. He has not dug up the bones of his ancestors in the Welsh mountains. He has stumbled on a Pharaoh in the land of the Egyptians . . . by making an exclusive secret of the contents of the inner tomb he has ranged against him the majority of the world's most influential newspapers.'

This was, unfortunately, true. But in fact Carnarvon was trying to protect his colleagues and himself from the necessity of coping with scores of journalists when every ounce of concentration was needed for their own unique task. This strained, tense atmosphere grew with the passing months, and eventually led to actions which might well have wrecked the greatest archaeological discovery ever made in Egypt.

An ivory gaming board and playing pieces

4 Desperation and Defeat

The king's court sandle with buckle in elaborate gold-work

Clearing of the Antechamber began on December 27, 1922, and was not completed until the middle of February, 1923—seven weeks of harassing, nerve-racking work in a room measuring only 25 ft. by 16 ft., containing over six hundred objects, many of them in a fragile condition. Some were so delicate that they had to be chemically treated on the spot, even before they were removed to the laboratory.

As Carter and his colleagues removed these things, one by one, their emotions were pulled first this way, then that. On the one hand it was their duty, as archaeologists, to photograph, record, preserve, and carefully transport each treasure from the tomb to the laboratory and thence to the Cairo Museum. But they were not merely transferring objects from one museum gallery to another; they were moving about in a room which no other human beings had seen for over three thousand years, and as they worked their way systematically from one end to the other, they found clear and dramatic evidence of what their predecessors had been up to. It was all very well to consider this as an intact sepulchre which had lain undisturbed for thirty centuries. It had, indeed, been miraculously preserved, unlike twenty-seven other royal burials in the Valley. But before the priests had sealed the doorway and left the tomb to silence and darkness, there had been some remarkable happenings within those walls.

For instance, one of the first objects to be examined was a brilliantly painted wooden casket. The outer surface had been prepared with gesso (a form of plaster), and on this the Ancient Egyptian artist had depicted lively

30

scenes showing the king hunting wild game, and battle scenes in which Tutankhamen, in his chariot, slays his traditional enemies, the Nubians and the Asiatics. These tableaux, with their delicacy of detail and harmony of colour, are reminiscent of Persian miniatures. But when they opened the lid Carter and his colleagues came upon a very odd medley of things.

Usually such boxes contain objects of one type, or at least of related types, but in this painted casket there were a pair of rush and papyrus sandals; a royal robe decorated with gold sequins and elaborate beadwork; other royal robes, one ornamented with three thousand golden rosettes; three more pairs of sandals worked in gold; a gilt headrest; an archer's gauntlet; various rolls and pads of cloth; and some articles of jewellery—all bundled together with the garments, which had not been neatly folded but stuffed into the box willy-nilly.

In another casket was a leopard-skin robe, such as used by priests, decorated with gold and silver stars, a buckle of sheet gold, a solid gold sceptre ornamented with lapis-lazuli glass, several necklaces, and a handful of heavy gold rings twisted up in a fold of linen. These rings had evidently formed part of a thief's intended loot. But why had they been put back in this box together with other ill-assorted articles?

Then there was a long ebony box at the top of which, just under the hinged lid, were shirts and underwear, all crumpled together. But underneath were sticks, bows, and a number of arrows, the points of which had been broken off for the sake of the metal. Thieves again. It soon became clear that originally these boxes had been neatly filled with objects of a similar kind; this one, for example, had contained bows and arrows. But when the chamber was tidied up by the priests after the robbers had left, the miscellaneous articles were gathered up from the floor and jammed, higgledy-piggledy, into the nearest available container.

The mounting of one of these sticks shows two captives, an Asiatic and a Negro—Egypt's traditional enemies of the North and South—

The plunderers' loot—eight gold rings tied in a fold of linen

31

The king's golden throne

bound together by the legs and forming the curved end of a walking stick. Their faces, hands, and feet are of ivory and ebony. Another similar stick has a handle in the form of a bound Negro captive. Some of the boxes still bore the original labels with inscriptions in hieratic (the Ancient Egyptian written form of hieroglyphs), detailing what was supposed to be inside. One, for instance stated that the box contained seventeen objects of lapis-lazuli blue. There were, in fact, sixteen vases inside, but in addition, carelessly packed, were a couple of boomerangs, a carved ivory casket, a wine-strainer, and the greater part of an elaborate corslet.

Everywhere there was evidence of attempted plunder followed by a hurried repacking and tidying up of the tomb's contents. The most prominent objects in the Antechamber were three magnificent couches of wood, plated with gold, ornamented with the heads of animals; a lioness, a hippopotamus, and a cow. Such heavy furniture could offer no attraction to the thieves, who had left them alone; but under one of the couches was something even more splendid, a glittering throne entirely covered with thick sheet gold, delicately inlaid with brilliantly coloured glass, faience, and semi-precious stones. The arms were shaped in the form of winged serpents—the royal cobra of Ancient Egypt—each wearing the Double Crown, symbolizing dominion over the South and North.

But what riveted the attention of the archaeologists was the scene inlaid on the back of the throne in red glass, blue faience, and calcite, glowing against a background of sheet gold. It was a scene in one of the rooms of Tutankhamen's palace. The young monarch is resting on a chair very like those found in his tomb. Standing before him is his equally young queen, Ankhesenamun, wearing an elaborate beaded collar, a long, elegant, semi-transparent robe of pleated linen, and a tall head-dress. She leans forward in a tender attitude, gently anointing the king's shoulder with perfumed oil from a vessel she holds in her left hand. The whole scene is charged with affection; these are royal

32

personages, almost weighed down by their trappings. Yet still they are human beings.

The work obviously belongs to what is called the Amarna Period of Egyptian art, a time when the Pharaoh Amenophis IV, who changed his name to Akhenaten, suddenly forbade the worship of the god Amun and the numerous other deities who had been revered in Egypt for more than fifteen hundred years. He tried to replace them by one sole god, whom he called the Aten, giver of life, and represented by the sun's disk with descending rays. You can see Akhenaten's god above the young couple. The object partly visible on the right is a round table, represented in such a way that you see both the sides and the top at once. The Egyptian artists ignored perspective.

But when Carter examined the legs of the throne, he found that the thieves had again been active. Several of the gold-encased struts had been snapped off; the plunderers would, of course, have taken the entire throne if they had had the chance, but fortunately for us they were prevented. How were they prevented? What had happened in that dark, cramped, rock-cut chamber some thirty centuries ago? How had the thieves got in? And having done

The back panel of the throne showing Tutankhamen and his wife Ankhesenamun

33

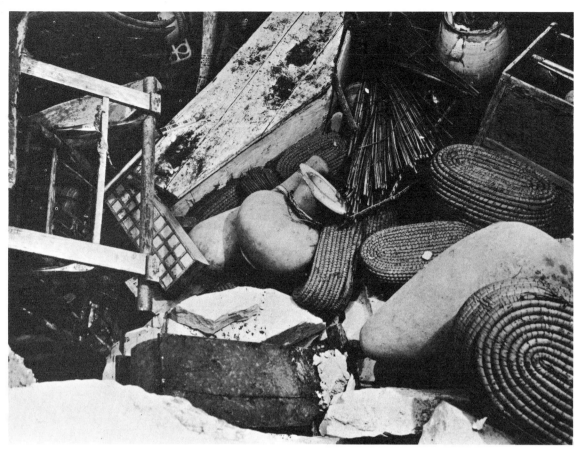

Interior of the Annex seen from the doorway.
The footprints of the tomb-robbers can be seen
upon the white bow box

so, and overturned so much in their frantic search for loot, why had they left so much behind, even to the handful of rings tied up in a piece of the royal linen?

They entered by tunnelling a hole through the rubble filling between the outer and inner doorways of the entrance corridor. Carter, long familiar with the habits of thieves, ancient and modern, detected this when he noticed that most of this rubble was clean and untouched, but that at one point, near the ceiling of the corridor the stones were dirty, indicating where the filling had been replaced when the tunnel had been filled in again. Having broken through the second sealed doorway the thieves had found themselves in the Antechamber, from which they had gained entrance to adjoining chambers by making holes in the partition walls.

34

One hole, in the wall beneath one of the great gilded couches, was still open; it had not been resealed by the Necropolis priests. Through it Carter saw a scene of utter confusion in the little room beyond. Alabaster vases, caskets, weapons, clothing, ornaments, were strewn over the floor and piled high against the walls. On a wooden bow case, still clearly visible, were the actual footprints of one of the thieves. The archaeologists, after a dismayed survey of this room, called the Annex, decided to postpone its clearance until the last.

Another hole, just wide enough to admit a small man (or woman) had been bored through the sealed entrance leading to the Burial Chamber, between the two sentinel figures. Penelope Fox, in her book, *Tutankhamen's Treasure*, remarks: 'A small breach had been made, which may or may not have been resealed anciently. . . .'

It is obvious that the thieves, who probably entered the tomb not long after the king's burial, could not have hoped to carry away the larger objects, even if they had had time. The tunnels were too small for that. They were after portable loot, especially precious metal, and they knew where to look for it. Their first action was to open the numerous boxes and toss their contents on to the floor. Then, in a frenzy of fearful haste, they tried to collect everything of value which they could carry away. One man found the gold rings. Snatching up a piece of the royal linen, he twisted the rings within its folds, made a knot, and probably stuffed the loot in his loincloth. Another man tore from its pedestal a small golden statue. A third snapped off the arrowheads, which were of valuable metal, and broke off the golden struts of the royal throne. The beautiful corslet, covered with golden sequins, was torn apart. Perhaps the thieves quarrelled and fought, blundering about in the semi-darkness, while the watchers at the far end of the tunnel shouted to them to be quick.

Then something happened; exactly what we

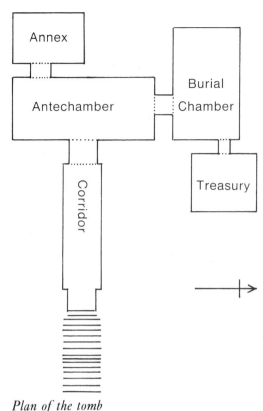

Plan of the tomb

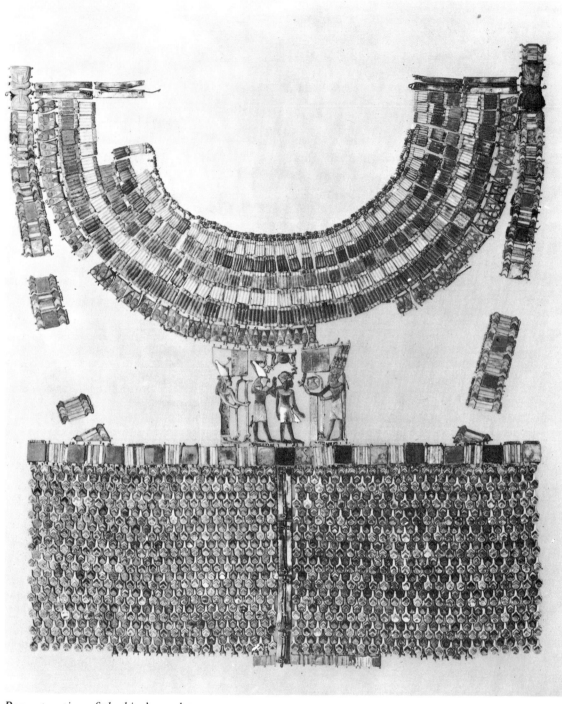

Reconstruction of the king's corslet

do not know. Either the robbers were trapped in the tomb by the guardians of the Necropolis, or, interrupted in their plundering, were forced to fly and were pursued. This is not mere speculation. The evidence was all too clear to the archaeologists as they examined the contents of the Antechamber. All that is uncertain is the outcome. The thieves left behind numerous objects of value which they could have taken, such as the gold rings found still wrapped in the scrap of linen in one of the boxes. On the other hand, some objects were missing. There is a strong possibility that some of the thieves got away, but that others were captured and forced to relinquish their loot. Some may have been trapped in the tomb itself, and their subsequent fate could not have been enviable.

Tomb robbers, ancient and modern, are the bane of the Egyptologist. But I suspect that Carter, despite his frustration, may have had a sneaking respect for those desperate men who had preceded him. Spurred on perhaps by hunger and poverty, they had defied not only the power of the state but—even more terrible— their own belief in the sanctity of the God-King, the Pharaoh, and violated his sepulchre. They failed, in this one instance; unhappily for them, but luckily for us.

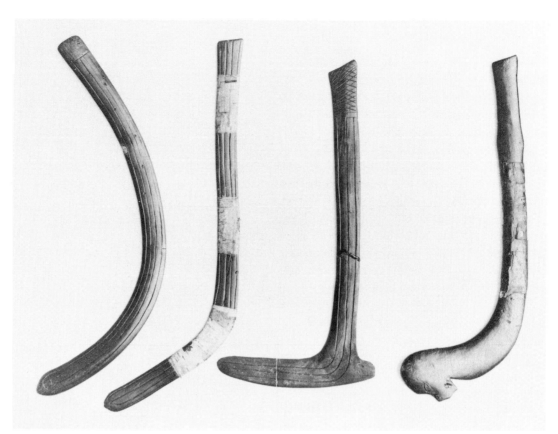

Weapons of offence: various boomerangs of hard wood decorated with bark.

One of the numerous baskets found discarded on the floor of the antechamber containing foodstuffs. These were mostly sundry foods and seeds including mandrake, grapes, dates, melon seeds and dom-nuts. Apart from oval baskets as illustrated, there were also round and bottle shaped examples, varying form 4 inches to 18 inches in their larger diameter.

Box on legs. Table-shaped cabinet about 23 inches high. Of plain dark red cedar wood panels with ebony uprights and stretchers encrusted with eulogistic titulary and other designations of the King in hieroglyphic script. The open work frieze symbolizes 'All Life and Good Fortune'.

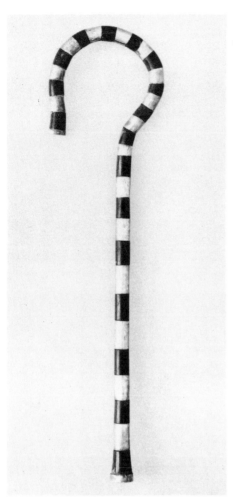

The King's sceptre of gold and lapis lazuli blue glass.

Detail of richly decorated bow case.

Scene in miniature upon the right-hand side of the lid of the painted casket. In the centre the King is represented in his chariot shooting desert fauna among which can be identified gazelle, hartebeest, wild ass, ostrich and striped hyena, fleeing before His Majesty's hounds. Behind the King are depicted his fan-bearers, courtiers and body-guard. In the field are depicted desert flora.

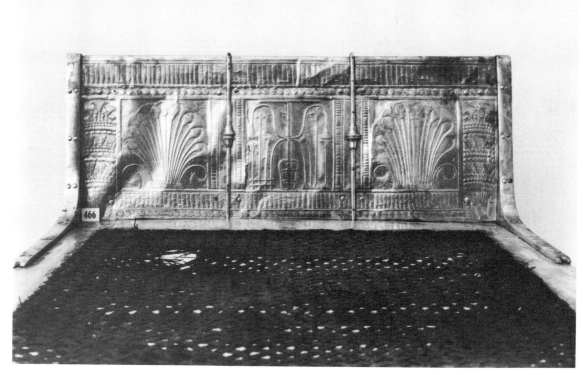

Detail of foot panel of gold-plated bedstead. Of carved ebony overlaid with sheet gold. The ornamentation is purely floral with garlands of petals and fruit, clumps of papyrus, etc., chased and embossed upon burnished gold.

Richly decorated dagger and sheath.

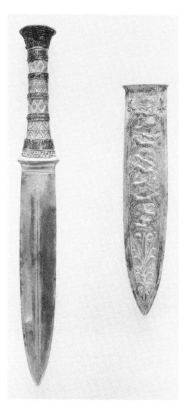

Scene upon front of painted casket. The King is depicted as a sphinx trampling upon his enemies. In the centre are the two cartouches of Tutankhamen.

Remains of two plaited linen-thread slings for hurling stones.

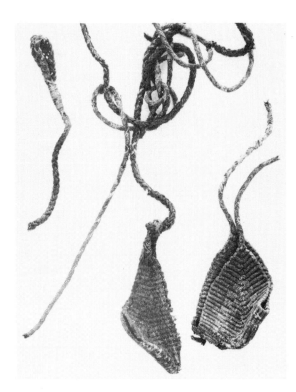

Fourth stage revealed in unpacking the casket. Visible are the remnants of garments, beads and various other items.

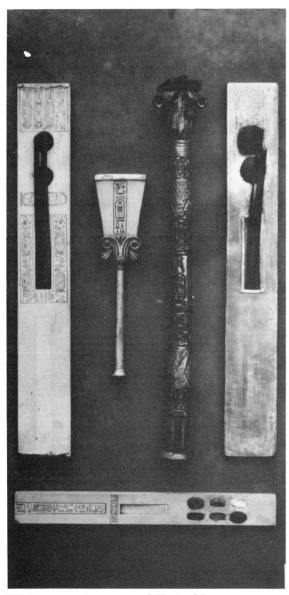

Writing implements of Tutankhamen, consisting of Mertaten's ivory palette, Tutankhamen's ivory and gold palettes, ivory burnisher and reed case.

'Birth of the Sun' pectoral ornament.

5 In the Presence of the King

The centre of the corslet represents Tutankhamen being introduced by a god and goddess to the Theban deity, Amun

It might be asked why it was that some of the objects needed artificial preservation whereas others did not. Obviously things made of stone, metal, or glass are less liable to be affected by humidity, dryness, or natural decay. One such is the lovely 'Wishing Cup'. It is of translucent alabaster, and is called 'lotiform' because the handle consists of lotus flowers supporting the emblem of eternal life. The hieroglyphic inscription gives the many titles of Tutankhamen and concludes: 'Live thy *Ka,* and mayst thou spend millions of years, thou lover of Thebes, sitting with thy face to the North Wind, and thine eyes beholding felicity.'

The wish 'mayst thou spend millions of years . . .' is fairly common in Egyptian tombs. The *ka* or spirit of the dead man was expected to spend more time living in the tomb or 'House of Eternity'. Egypt being a very hot country, one of the greatest pleasures is to sit out of doors in the evening and enjoy the north wind. That is what the King's *ka* wished to do.

The wooden articles in the Antechamber, of sound timber and well carpentered, were usually in fair condition, but had shrunk. When they were plated with gold and inlaid with delicate mosaics, this caused difficulty. The shrinkage left a gap between the wood and the covering, the tiny pieces of glass, lapis, carnelian etc. tended to break away, and Carter had to resort to melted paraffin wax to hold everything together. It was even worse with the fabrics. If these had been neatly folded before being put in the boxes they might have survived, or at least the gold sequins and other ornaments sewn on to them would have been found in

38

Tutankhamen's wishing cup

their correct relative positions. But this was
rarely the case. The garments had been jammed
into the caskets, and mixed up with various
items of hardware; humidity (of which we shall
speak later) had caused the linen to disintegrate
to the point where it fell apart at a touch.
Then there were the beads—hundreds of
thousands of them—which had been inlaid into
the beautiful pectorals (breast-ornaments) and
other golden jewellery, or made up the many-
tiered necklaces, collarets, and bracelets of
which the Egyptians were so fond. Many of
these beads were scattered in confusion, but in
other cases, by careful scrutiny the archaeologists were able to note and record where they

Collar as found resting on the lid of a box

had fallen; then came the tedious operation of stringing them together on new threads.

For certain reasons—partly the seepage of water through the porous rock, partly the decomposition of organic matter within the tomb—dampness had, at some time, attacked some of the objects. For instance at the southern end of the Antechamber, near the door, were the dismembered remains of a number of chariots; the axles had been sawn apart to get the vehicles into the tomb, but the wheels, body-work and poles were all intact, and richly plated with gold. They have since been reconstructed, but the harness had to be replaced. The leather of the original one had decomposed into a black, viscid mass due to humidity.

These chariots (others were found in the Treasury adjoining the burial chamber), were among the most interesting objects found in an Egyptian royal tomb. Many pictures of them existed, and some examples had been found, namely in the tomb of Yuya and Thuya discovered by Theodore Davis. But these chariots

40

Reconstruction of the collar

of Tutankhamen were the first royal examples
ever found. His name was on them, of course,
together with gold-embossed panels depicting
the usual bound Nubian and Asiatic captives.
The chariot, though used for hunting, was
primarily an instrument of war, and a deadly one.
Some Pharaohs, such as Ramesses II, led
their armies into battle from chariots, and
the chariot arm of the Egyptian army was
probably roughly equivalent to the swift light-
armoured tanks of modern times. Its great

41

A jewelled boss on the second state chariot

advantage was mobility. There were two-man chariots, one man driving, the other shooting arrows, but those found in Tutankhamen's tomb seem to have been designed only for one driver.

They were light, but strongly built. They had no springs (which had not been invented), but the driver stood so far back that road shocks were absorbed partly by the pole, and the floor was a webbing which gave a certain amount of resilience. The six-spoked wheels were beautifully made—tough, light and springy; the tyres were covered with leather. No seat was provided, and the vehicle was open at the back so that the driver could leap down quickly when necessary. Drawn by two powerful horses, the Egyptian chariot must have been a tricky thing to handle, especially at high speed, and even more difficult to shoot from. I imagine that the young king, whose sporting interests are obvious from other objects found in his tomb, was trained in both arts from an early age.

One of the most fascinating aspects of the whole discovery was the revelation, in the objects found, of ritual and religious formality combined with touches of simple humanity. Many of the treasures had been specially made to accompany Tutankhamen in the life beyond the tomb; others had clearly been things he had used and treasured in life—the great number of bows, for instance, and nearly three hundred arrows of differing types. Also he seems to have been a keen collector of sticks, some simple, some embellished with gold. There was one simple reed, the mounting of which bore the inscription: 'A reed cut by His Majesty's own hand,' and tucked under one of the couches was a tiny chair, too small to have been used by anyone but a child. There was also a sling with pebbles, and a number of games played with 'men' on a squared surface.

Here was a sepulchre of the mighty Pharaoh, Lord of the Two Lands (Egypt was once two Kingdoms, the South and the North), son of Re the sun-god; a divine ruler who had been buried

42

with pomp, with solemnity, and accompanied with immeasurable wealth, as befitted his royal power and divine nature. Yet it was also the tomb of a human boy with a boy's interests. There was evidence, too, of a personal tenderness standing out all the more vividly and movingly by contrast with the solemn splendour of the funerary equipment. There were simple floral wreaths leaning against the wall, perhaps placed there by the girl-queen, Ankhesenamun. Carter admits that at first it seemed a sacrilege to touch these tributes.

Gradually, methodically, with meticulous care, Carter, Callender, Mace, Lythgoe and the rest removed each precious artefact from the Antechamber, having first made certain that all future generations of archaeologists would have a complete pictorial record showing where each object had stood. The room was empty, save for the two guardian figures in black and gold, and a heap of sticks—probably arrows—which, together with a circular wicker basket, were piled against the lower part of the wall covering the breach made by the ancient tomb robbers. This heap of miscellaneous objects can be clearly seen in the photograph which Burton took to illustrate the cleared Antechamber.

At the risk of appearing to digress I would like to draw attention to this heap, which has long puzzled me. Carter states in his book, *The Tomb of Tut-ankh-amen*, that 'close examination revealed the fact that a small breach had been made near the bottom, just wide enough to admit a boy or a slightly-built man, and that the hole had subsequently been filled up and resealed.' Carter also published a photograph showing this resealed hole; in it the darker-coloured plaster shows clearly where it had been refilled. This plaster also bears the familiar seal of the Necropolis.

In the chapter describing preparations for opening the door Carter writes: 'By the middle of February our work in the Antechamber was finished. With the exception of the two sentinel statues, left for a special reason, all its contents had been removed to the laboratory, every inch

A small chair, probably used by the king when a child, carved of ebony and inlaid with ivory and gold

43

*The photograph taken to illustrate the cleared
Antechamber*

of its floor had been swept and sifted for the
last bead or fallen piece of inlay, and it now stood
bare and empty.'

In Burton's picture the couches have been
removed; so has the painted casket which stood
in front of the heap of arrows. Why, one asks,
had they not also been removed when Carter's
photograph was taken? Why were they left
concealing the robbers' hole which, according
to Burton's photograph had been blocked up
and impressed with the seal of the Necropolis,
exactly like those on the untouched part of the
wall? Again, Carter's photograph shows that the
resealed portion was distinctly darker than the
rest. Would plaster have retained such a
distinct contrast in coloration after three
thousand years? It is curious, particularly as
the other robbers' hole, between the Antechamber and the Annex, had been left open.

44

It is possible, of course, that the priests responsible for clearing up the tomb took the precaution of resealing the hole leading to the burial chamber, the most sacred part of the sepulchre, but the matter remains a mystery.

On February 17, 1923, when an official party including Lord Carnarvon, Lady Evelyn Herbert, the Minister of Public Works, the Director-General of the Antiquities Service, and some twenty other personages attended the opening, the lower part of the wall was concealed behind a wooden platform built to enable Carter and his assistants to reach the topmost level of the sealed doorway when they began to demolish it. The official party, seated on chairs in the now-empty Antechamber, watched while Carter began work, first searching for the wooden lintel above the door, and then slowly and painstakingly removing the stone filling, being

Part of the sealed doorway showing the reclosing of the plunderers' hole at the bottom

Carter and Mace at the opening of the sealed doorway

careful to see that none of the blocks fell inward into the chamber beyond.

Carter wrote, of this moment: '. . . after about ten minutes I had made a hole large enough to enable me to . . . insert an electric torch. An astonishing sight it revealed, for there, within a yard of the doorway, stretching as far as one could see and blocking the entrance to the chamber, stood what to all appearance was a solid wall of gold. . . . We were at the entrance of the actual burial-chamber of the king, and that which barred our way was the side of an immense gilt shrine built to cover and protect the sarcophagus. It was visible now from the Antechamber by the light of the standard lamps, and as stone after stone was removed, and its

46

gilded surface came gradually into view, we could, as though by an electric current, feel the tingle of excitement which thrilled the spectators behind the barrier.'

The twenty or so human beings watching from the Antechamber were to have an experience which no one of our time, and probably no one in three thousand years, has ever known: to be the first to enter the burial chamber of a Pharaoh lying exactly as he was laid out over three thousand years ago, surrounded by all his resplendent panoply of death. One of them, Sir Alan Gardiner, gave me this eyewitness account.

'We had seen such shrines depicted in ancient papyri, but this was the real thing. There it was, splendid in its blue and gold, and almost filling the entire space of the second chamber. It reached nearly to the ceiling, and the space between it and the walls at the sides was not more than about two feet.

'First Carter and Carnarvon went in, squeezing their way through the narrow space, and we waited for them to return. When they came back they both lifted their hands in amazement at what they had seen. . . . When it came to my turn I went in with Professor Breasted. We pushed our way through and then turned left, so that we were opposite the front of the shrine, which had two great doors. Carter had drawn the bolt and opened these doors, so that we could see that inside the great outer shrine, which was 17 ft. long and 11 ft. wide, was another, smaller shrine, also with double doors, with the seal still unbroken. In fact there were in all four of these gilded shrines, one inside the other like a Chinese nest of boxes, and within the fourth was the sarcophagus and the coffins, which we were not to see until a year later.'

Sir Alan went on: 'If you go to the Cairo Museum today you can see these objects. They are still magnificent, of course, but some of the gold has a slightly tarnished appearance. Now when we first entered the tomb the gold shrines glittered with the greatest possible brilliancy. . . . Beyond the Burial Chamber we found on the right the entrance to another room. . . . It was

The shrine within the sepulchre

47

Opening the doors of the fourth and innermost shrine

48

full of marvels. There was the King's canopic chest [containing the internal organs removed during embalmment] guarded by four delicate little golden goddesses, two of whom were looking over their shoulders towards us as if in protest at our intrusion. There were more golden chariots, a great shrouded effigy of the jackal-god Anubis, guardian of the cemeteries; and there were many other precious things, including a number of chests, boxes and caskets. Carter opened one of these and on the top lay a beautiful ostrich-feather fan. The feathers were perfect, fluffing out just as if they had been recently plucked, and waving gently in the slight draught which came through the now-opened doorway of the sepulchre. Those feathers completely annihilated the centuries for me. It was just as if the king had been buried only a few days before. Of course in a few days they began to decay and had to be preserved in paraffin wax, but when I first saw them they were perfect; and they made on me an impression such as I had never experienced before, and never shall again.'

The doors of the second and third shrines were bolted with ebony bolts shot into metal staples and fastened in the centre with cord tied to metal staples and sealed

6 The Quarrel and the 'Curse'

The back pendant of the corslet depicting the winged Kheper beetle supporting the solar disk

I have mentioned that Carter was not the least irritable of men, and he had to cope with problems which would have tried the nerves of any conscientious archaeologist. There was the unceasing stream of visitors sent by the Egyptian Government; there were the eager reporters gathered round the tomb entrance every day, resentful of the fact that only the correspondent of *The Times* was allowed within the sepulchre during actual excavations. There was tension between Carter and Carnarvon themselves, for reasons which I have explained—mainly the fact that Carnarvon believed that, under the terms of the concession granted him by the Egyptian Government, a proportion of the finds belonged to him. With this Carter violently disagreed, saying that all the treasures were rightly the property of Egypt and should remain there.

In February, 1923, Carter quarrelled with his old friend and patron; there was an angry scene, after which, according to Charles Breasted, the son of James Breasted, 'Carter requested Carnarvon to leave his house and never enter it again.' Soon after this Lord Carnarvon came down with fever brought on by an infected insect-bite. Pneumonia set in, and on April 5, 1923, Carnarvon died, at the age of fifty-seven. Immediately the newspapers of the world sensationalized this as 'the Pharaoh's curse' and even went so far as to say that Carnarvon had pricked his finger on some object left deliberately in the tomb by its guardians.

The so-called 'curse of Pharaoh' has become a legend, and legends, once established, tend to stick. But what are the facts? Ten years after

50

the opening of the tomb all but one of the five who first entered it were still alive. Carter survived till 1939, dying at the age of sixty-six. Burton, the photographer, and Rex Engelbach, Chief Inspector of Antiquities, and later Director of the Cairo Museum, also lived the normal span of years. Lady Evelyn Herbert, now Lady Beauchamp, is, at the time of writing, still alive. Dr. Derry, who performed the dissection of the Pharaoh's mummy (and should therefore be especially accursed) live to be over eighty. Sir Alan Gardiner died in December, 1963, in his eighties.

In fact the 'curse' is pure nonsense, and should be regarded as such. But the legend is now so well established that even in 1954, when I had contracted dengue fever in Egypt and, as a result, developed a lame knee for a few weeks, an English newspaper came out with the headline: 'BBC Producer and Author Cursed by the Pharaoh (I happened to mention to a journalist friend that I had spent some time watching the excavation of a Pharaonic pyramid!).

People who heed such fanciful stuff must have starved imaginations. The real facts about Tutankhamen's tomb are much more romantic than any fiction. For instance, let us look at the real story of what happened after the opening of the Second Chamber containing the great gilded shrines and the three coffins. During the season 1923 to 1924, work was concentrated on dismantling and removing the four golden shrines which occupied almost the entire space of the burial chamber. This was a task which taxed Carter's ingenuity to the utmost, but in the end the shrines were taken apart without damage and removed to Cairo. On February 14, 1924, in the presence of leading officials, the lid of the quartzite sarcophagus, which lay within the innermost shrine, was raised, and the onlookers saw for the first time the splendid outer coffin of the Pharaoh, of wood plated with gold and inlaid with semi-precious stones.

And on the very same day the following notice appeared in the principal hotels in Luxor:

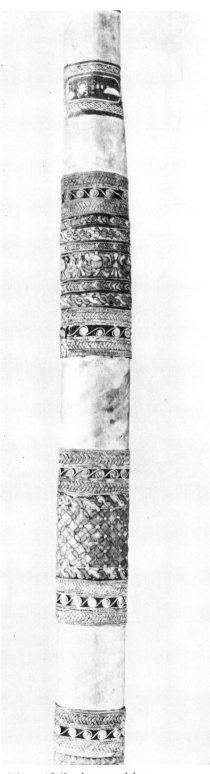

A beautifully decorated bow

51

Another of the king's ear-rings

'Owing to the impossible restriction and discourtesies on the part of the Public Works Department and its Antiquities Service, all my collaborators in protest have refused to work any further upon the scientific investigation of the discovery of the Tomb of Tutankhamen. I am therefore obliged to make known to the public that immediately after the Press view of the tomb this morning between 10.00 A.M. and noon the tomb will be closed and no further work carried out.'

(Signed) HOWARD CARTER

This was the culmination of Carter's dispute with the Egyptian Government. The crux of his complaints was that by harassing him with minute instructions as to the manner in which he conducted the work, and by sending him streams of visitors, the Government had made it impossible for him to carry out his delicate and exacting task. In this he was fully supported by his colleagues, American and British. One of them, Breasted, wrote in his book, *Pioneer to the Past*: 'The scientific men agreed that, however injudicious and temperamental his behaviour had been at times . . . the Egyptian Government's treatment had been so inconsiderate as to have forced remonstrative action upon him.'

The effect of this announcement was immediate. The Government took over the tomb, reopened it to visitors, and invited large numbers of officials and their wives to see it. A British journalist who watched these proceedings, which were rounded off by fireworks, commented at the time in the *Egyptian Gazette*: 'A pathetic note was provided by two of Mr. Carter's trusted Egyptian foremen, faithfully guarding a heap of their master's property, not far from the mouth of the tomb for the discovery of which they had served him with such unflagging fidelity and perseverance. Their saddened faces left no doubt as to their thoughts at seeing the careless throng passing into the tomb which, to them and their master, represented the almost sacred crowning of the labour of a lifetime.'

The goddess Selkit, one of the four guardian goddesses carved in high relief on each of the four corners of the sarcophagus

A ceremonial baton

It is worth noticing here that the workmen were almost certainly 'Qufti', that is from the village of Quft in Upper Egypt. The distinguished British excavator Sir Flinders Petrie had recruited most of his workmen from this village before Carter's time, and even to this day the best and most reliable Egyptian workmen, trained for archaeological 'digs', usually come from this village. When I was watching the late Zakaria Goneim excavating a buried pyramid in 1954, his *reis* or foremen were Qufts.

In his book *The Tomb of Tut-ankh-amen* Carter reprints a moving letter in imperfect English from his head man, sent to him at the time when he was prevented by officialdom from re-entering the tomb. It is well worth reprinting here, since it provides such a striking contrast between the loyalty and affection of the trained Egyptian archaeological helper, who has probably spent his life (from the days when he was a mere 'basket-boy', carrying debris in baskets) in helping European and American excavators do their scientific work, and the minor government officials who, like most government officials everywhere, are over concerned with rules and regulations. The letter reads:

'Honourable Sir,

Beg to write this letter hoping you are enjoying good health, and ask the Almighty to keep you and bring you back to us in safety. Beg to inform you that Store No. 15 is alright, Treasure is alright, the Northern Store is alright, Wadain and House is alright, and in all your work order is carried on according to your honourable instructions. Reis Hussein, Gad Hassan, Hassan Awad Abdelal Ahmed and all the *ghaffirs* of the house beg to send their best regards.

My best regards to your honourable self.

Longing to your early coming,

Your obedient servant,

REIS AHMED GURGAR'

It is more than probable that Carter would never have been allowed to return to the tomb but for the tragedy of the assassination of a

54

senior British Officer, Sir Lee Stack, in November, 1924. In the meantime Carter had fought a lawsuit with the Egyptian Government but without success. But from the moment the murderer shot Sir Lee Stack on the doorstep of his home in Cairo, such was the anger aroused in British Government circles that the British, who had up to that time been relinquishing their hold on Egyptian affairs, re-established firm control. As an indirect result the legal conflicts concerning the Tomb of Tutankhamen were forgotten, and Carter was allowed to return.

Reis Ahmed Gurgar, Reis Hussein, Gad Hassan, Hassan Awad Abdelal Ahmed and the rest of his faithful *ghaffirs* were waiting when their master returned. The iron grille swung open, and once again Carter was in the presence of the dead Pharaoh, still lying in the innermost of the three coffins, the outer of which could be seen under the plate-glass screen which Carter had placed there for its protection. The

The first outermost coffin within the sarcophagus after the linen shrouds had been removed

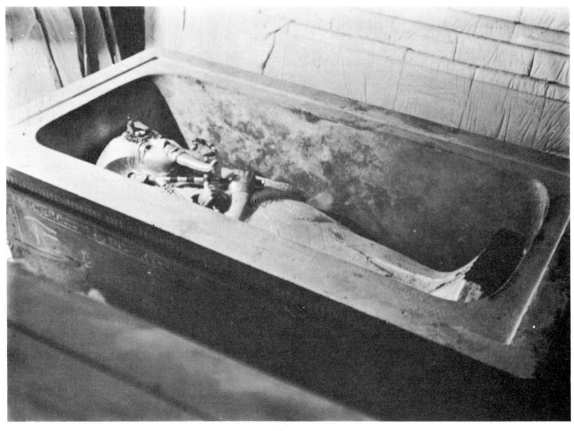

55

footsteps of the great archaeologist and his helpers echoed in the rock-cut chamber.

Of this moment Carter wrote in his book: 'Once more we entered the Burial Chamber. Once more our powerful electric lamps lit up the great quartzite sarcophagus. Under the plate-glass screen . . . was revealed the gold-encased outer coffin that seems to gather power of appealing to the emotions the moment it is seen. With the shadows of the ancient gods there can be no vulgar intimacy. . . .'

But there was one bitter moment for Carter. When the burial chamber had first been disclosed a delicate linen pall had been found draped over the inner shrine (the one which enclosed the outermost of the three coffins). Carter had had to remove it in order to dismantle the shrine and get at the sarcophagus. But in his absence the Egyptian officials, instead of replacing the pall within the tomb, where it would have been safe, had left it exposed to the fierce summer sun in an improvised shed or shelter outside. When Carter returned, all that remained of this unique piece of three-thousand-year-old fabric were a few rapidly decaying fragments. A newspaper commentator of the time wrote: 'Mr. Carter's agitation was intense, but he contented himself with one remark:

"Well, anyway, it was your Pall, not mine . . . and it *was* the only one in the world." '

An openwork design on one of the chariots

56

7 The Three Coffins

It may be helpful at this stage to remember what Sir Alan Gardiner, one of the fortunate few who were privileged to enter the burial chamber at its first opening said about it: 'We had seen such things in ancient papyri, but here was the real thing.'

The Ancient Egyptians were fond of depicting, on the walls of their tombs, especially the tombs of non-royal personages, scenes familiar to them in their everyday life. For instance in the tomb of a great official named Rekhmire, at Thebes, there is a scene showing workmen making what we call 'funerary equipment' that is, shrines, statuary and the like intended for a royal burial. Rekhmire happened to be Superintendent of the Royal Workshops of the God Amun, and in the tomb paintings he is shown overseeing the labours of his workmen, some of whom are making caskets, vases, and even a statue of King Tuthmosis III (one of Tutankhamen's predecessors) for the approval of their master. That is what Sir Alan meant by 'We had seen such things'—not only in ancient papyri (which were his particular study) but on the walls of tombs. The discovery of Tutankhamen's sepulchre, enthralling though it was, did not have such elements of the *unknown* as excited the world when Heinrich Schliemann discovered the graves of hitherto-unknown kings and queens at Mycenae in Greece, or when Sir Arthur Evans in 1899, came upon the remains of a great Palace at Knossos in Crete dating from before 2000 B.C. There were no written or pictorial records of such places, whereas in Ancient Egypt there were.

But, until Carter found the burial of Tutan-

An example of sculpture on the walls of a tomb of a noble of the Eighteenth Dynasty. He is shown with his wife seated before an offering table

khamen, no human being had ever set eyes on the royal coffins of a Pharaoh, intact, undisturbed by robbers, standing within the nest of gold-encased wooden shrines as they had been placed in the narrow chamber more than thirty centuries ago. You may be surprised by the word 'coffins' in the plural. Why more than one coffin? We do not know, except that there may have been some religious meaning in the actual number of protective devices surrounding the body of the king, who was also a god.

Dr. Margaret Murray, the distinguished archaeologist and anthropologist who died in 1963 at the age of one hundred years, once pointed out to me that, to the ancient peoples, seven was a 'lucky number'. There were four outer shrines protecting the coffins, and three inner coffins, each nesting within the other; seven in all. Whether this was coincidental or deliberate we shall probably never know.

The third (innermost) coffin of gold covered with the linen shroud and floral collarette, as it lay in the shell of the second coffin

So Carter began the last stage of his task, the opening of the three coffins, each enclosed within the next. The opening of these coffins taxed all Carter's resourcefulness. They nested within each other so tightly, he tells us, that it was not possible to pass one's little finger between them. Moreover the funeral libations poured over them at the time of interment had solidified like cement. The problem was to remove the inner coffins without damaging the delicate inlay of carnelian and lapis-lazuli, set within tiny semicircles of gold which shimmered like the scales of a fish.

Of these tense weeks Carter wrote: 'Everything may seem to be going well when suddenly you hear a crack. Little pieces of surface ornament fall. Your nerves are at an almost painful tension. What is happening? All available room in the narrow space is crowded with your men. What is needed to avert a catastrophe?'

Thanks to Carter's patience and engineering skill all these problems were overcome. The second and third (inner) coffins were removed from the large outer one with all their blazonry of gold leaf, carnelian and lapis. Each was of 'anthropoid' shape, i.e., in the form of a mummified human body, and each had on its lid a representation of the boy king, his arms crossed upon his breast and carrying the twin insignia of Ancient Egyptian royalty, the crook and the flail. And on each coffin was represented the head of the Pharaoh wearing the 'false beard', the wig and royal head-dress surmounted by two more symbols on the brow; the cobra or uraeus, representing Lower Egypt, and the vulture, representing dominion over Upper Egypt.

Such symbols of majesty had been worn on the crown of the Pharaohs for more than one thousand years before Tutankhamen was born, and were a memory of the far-distant period, before 3000 B.C., when Egypt was divided into two Kingdoms, the North and the South.

Within the second coffin lay the third and last, and this, when revealed, filled the discoverers with awe. For it was of solid gold, so

59

The solid gold innermost coffin which contained the mummy

heavy that it needed four men to lift it. The lid represented the Pharaoh in all his splendid regalia. The face was a portrait; below it his crossed arms held, again, the sacred crook and flail. The goldwork was the masterpiece of a craftsman of genius. Inlaid within the shining metal was a shimmering pattern of carnelian and lapis, each tiny stone inset with the utmost care.

Below the crossed arms, incised on the gold, were representations of two lovely goddesses, each with wings which enfolded the body of the young Pharaoh, as if to protect him. The discoverers gazed, astonished, at this revelation, and it seemed to Carter, as he says in his book, that 'we were in the presence of the dead king, and must do him reverence.'

It is not easy to imagine the mixed feelings of those privileged to make this discovery. They had stumbled upon the intact burial of a Pharaoh, the only one ever found in his original coffin and tomb. The priests of those far-off times, had taken fantastic precautions to guard and protect the royal body, even though, as we shall see, Tutankhamen was only a minor king, almost the last of a declining and unpopular dynasty.

And here stood the scientific excavators of the twentieth century, torn between respect and awe for the long-dead king, and curiosity about the body which lay within the golden inner coffin. Was the body well preserved, like that of Seti I and Ramesses III? Would it be possible, once the mummy wrappings were removed, to look on the actual features of Tutankhamen? There could be no doubt concerning the outcome. The second and inner coffins were carried from the tomb to that of Seti I, which still served Carter and his colleagues as a laboratory, the lid was removed, and the final work of unwrapping was begun. The surgeon and anatomist, Dr. Derry, stood by to perform an autopsy or 'post-mortem' on the royal corpse, just as if it was a body of recent date, and not that of the ruler of Egypt more than three thousand years ago.

Science is remorseless.

60

8 The Pharaoh is Revealed

The lid of the gold coffin was secured to its base by tongues sliding into grooves. When the archaeologists removed the lid, in the brilliant electric light installed in Seti's tomb, there lay before them the elaborately wrapped mummy of the Pharaoh and the most wonderful sight of all, a golden portrait head of the young monarch, inlaid with blue lapis and wearing the royal cobra and vulture on its brow, as on the outer coffins. From the photograph you can get some idea of this superb example of the Ancient Egyptian goldsmith's art by some unknown artist who is worthy to stand beside Cellini and any of the finest goldsmiths of the Renaissance.

Having recovered from their astonishment, the next problem facing the archaeologists was that of removing the mummy from under the mask, and this proved extremely difficult, as, when the body had been laid in the coffin more than three thousand years ago, funeral libations had been poured over it and these, solidifying, had attached the mask to the coffin, as firmly as strong glue. Not only that, but the same libations (Carter estimated that two bucketsful of liquid had been poured in) had caused the inner, gold coffin to adhere to the second, wooden coffin.

Here indeed was a problem; how to separate the two coffins and remove the gold mask. The excavators first tried exposing them to the fierce Egyptian sun, but to no effect. Carter's final solution, a masterpiece of ingenuity, will be studied later. Meanwhile Dr. Douglas Derry, set about unwrapping the mummy, removing it from under the gold mask, and then examining

Profile view of the mask of Tutankhamen

61

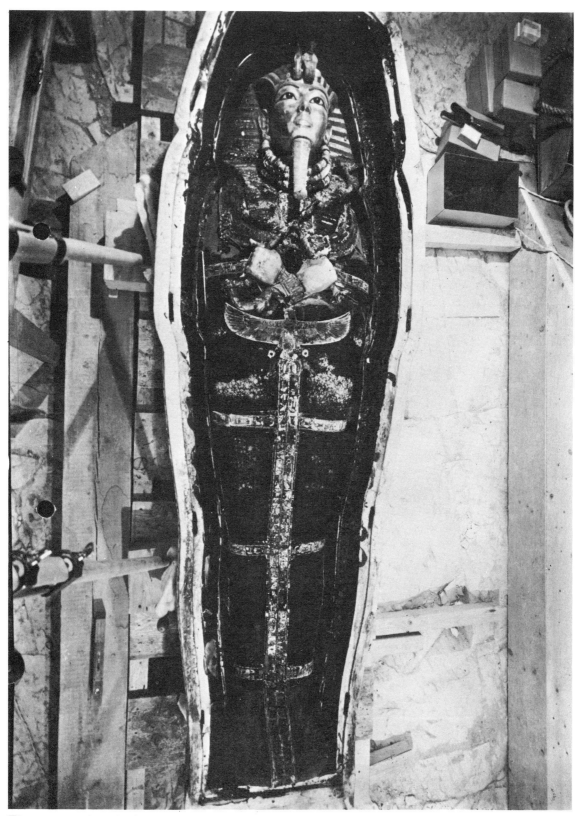

The mummy of the king as first seen

the bones. Here is his own account, which he recorded for me in 1949.

'Over the head and shoulders, reaching down to the middle of the body, was a solid gold mask representing an effigy of the young king. . . . This mask was firmly stuck to the floor of the coffin by certain resinated materials . . . the mummy was glued to the floor and it was some days before I was able to release the body and draw the head and shoulders out ot the mask which remained stuck to the bottom of the coffin by the rock-like hardness of the dried resins. . . . As the one who actually unwrapped the mummy of the King the supposed curse should rest most heavily on me, and I should have been the first to die. But I've survived it 26 years and I am now 74.'

Actually Dr. Derry lived on into his 'eighties.

As each layer of mummy wrappings was removed it was seen that the Pharaoh's body was bedizened with more gold and jewellery. Necklaces of gold and semi-precious stones encircled his neck: his fingers gleamed with gold rings; even his fingernails and toenails were fitted with tiny gold sheaths. Around his slender body were trappings of heavy gold plaques bearing welcoming speeches by gods and goddesses addressed to the young king—he was probably about seventeen or eighteen when he died—as he entered the Underworld to join his fellow dieties. According to Egyptian belief the Pharaoh was the son of Re, god of the sun, and would, on his death, join the gods.

These greetings are extremely moving and beautiful. The goddess Nut (pronounced Newt) thus addresses him:

'I reckon thy beauties, O Osiris, King Kheperu-Neb-Re; thy soul liveth; thy veins are firm. Thou smellest the air and goeth out as a God, going out as Atum, O Osiris, Tutankhamun. . . .'

And Geb, god of the Earth, says to him:

'My beloved son, inheritor of the throne of

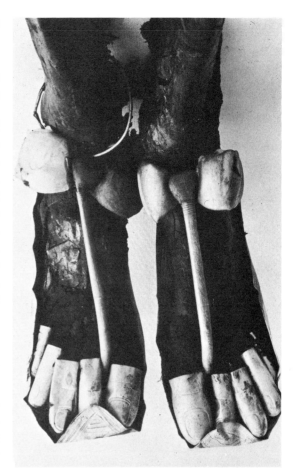

The feet were encased in gold sandals and the toes were adorned with gold sheaths

63

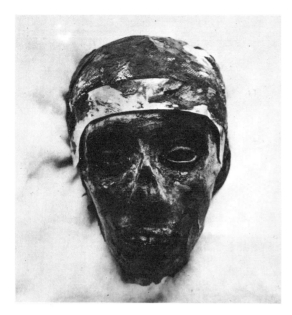

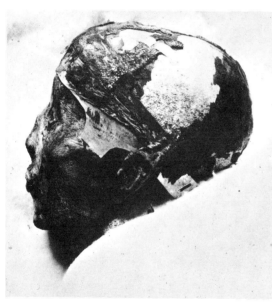

The head of the mummy

Osiris, the King Kheperu-Neb-Re; thy nobility is perfect; thy Royal Palace is powerful; . . . thy stability is in the mouth of the living; O Osiris, Tutankhamun. . . .'

What was the meaning of these inscriptions, of which there were several others? They were magical spells which were believed to assure the king's immortality. Osiris was the Egyptian God of the Dead and Judge of Souls, originally, but after a time every king (and indeed everyone who could afford a tomb) became '*an* Osiris' followed by his name. Incidentally Kheperu-Neb-Re (or in some readings Neb-Kheperu-Re) was one of the royal names, of which Tutankhamen was another. Notice particularly the emphasis on the physical preservation of the body . . . 'thy veins are firm' etc. In another text occur the words, 'Thy heart is in thy body eternally'. This was very important, because to the Ancient Egyptians the heart, not the brain, was the centre of intelligence and feeling.

When the pathetic little body was finally revealed, it proved to be that of a mere boy in his late 'teens; the skull was not as well preserved as that of some royal mummies, but sufficient remained to satisfy the anatomist that the unknown genius who made the golden mask had faithfully portrayed the features of the dead Pharaoh. The cause of his early death remains unknown.

The next problem was the removal of the sumptuous solid-gold coffin from the second, wooden one, in such a way as not to damage either. Carter eventually decided to line the interior of the gold coffin with zinc plates, and then, supporting the two coffins, on trestles, upside down, over several paraffin stoves, he succeeded in melting the resins so that the two could be separated. But it was a tricky operation. The wooden coffin was covered with blankets saturated with water, and Carter had to regulate the temperature of the paraffin stoves so that the heat never approached the melting point of zinc (520 degrees Centigrade, 968 degrees Farenheit).

Finally the first, or outer wooden coffin, which had been left within the sarcophagus, was lifted out by hoisting tackle slung from overhead scaffolding. This too, was accomplished without damage to the coffin, which now stands in the Egyptian Museum in Cairo, together with the inner, golden coffin and the mask. When all the work was over, the body of the king was laid reverently in its second coffin and replaced within the sarcophagus in the tomb, where it still lies today.

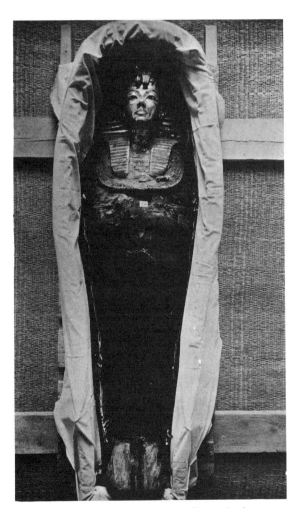

The royal mummy within its coffin with the external wrappings removed

9 Romance and Reality

One of the king's gaming boards

There is in this fantastic story elements of high romance and earthy reality. It is almost heartbreaking—the contrast between the splendour of the God-King, surrounded by all his panoply of wealth and power, walking into the sunlight of immortality, welcomed by his fellow gods, and the huddle of bones within the mummy wrappings being scientifically examined by an anatomist. Surely not two worlds could seem more opposite in character than our own and that of Ancient Egypt. The elaborate precautions taken by the Egyptians to protect the body of their monarch, the custom of burying with him such riches as truly befit the words 'a King's ransom'; the belief in magical spells and the efficacy of paintings and sculpture, not as objects of art, but as tokens of one's wealth and an assurance that one would continue to enjoy it in the next world—contrast all this with our own comparative indifference to the fate of our earthly bodies, our reliance not on magical spells but on scientifically established fact. What a difference!

And yet, in many ways the Ancient Egyptians, for all their strange beliefs, were very like us. Take the objects found in Tutankhamen's tomb. Among the golden splendour were ordinary human things: a child's games and toys; a 'keepsake' in the form of a lock of hair from the head of Queen Tiye. Again there is the clear evidence of tenderness and affection between the young king and his queen Ankhesenamun, both little more than children, as we see on the relief which adorns the back of the Throne. Among the golden regalia were the bodies of two stillborn children, each in its little

66

coffin, evidence that Ankhesenamun had twice tried to bear a child. Probably—almost certainly in fact—she was left a childless widow, which has important bearing on the story we shall tell in the last chapter of this book.

Coming to our own scientific world, we have nothing of which we need feel ashamed concerning the excavation of Tutankhamen's burial, except for the vulgar and unnecessary disputes which accompanied it, and which might have brought the whole operation into jeopardy. If the tomb had been discovered by the ordinary Egyptian 'illicit-digger' or tomb robber, certainly a few of the more valuable objects would have come on to the market, but many would have been destroyed for the sake of the gold, and much valuable historical information would have been lost forever, as it was in the case of all the other royal burials.

As it happened, thanks to the determination, skill and perseverance of Carter and Lord Carnarvon, this unique discovery—and there is unlikely ever to be another one—was carried out under the strictest scientific control. Experts from Britain and the United States readily gave their services, and the result is that nowadays every visitor to Cairo can wander through a suite of galleries containing all the objects found in the tomb, displayed in full splendour and protected against decay.

Two men in particular should be commended for this: one is the late Rex Engelbach, an Englishman, formerly Director of the Museum, who was mainly responsible for arranging and displaying the objects; the other is A. Lucas, a chemist and one-time scientific adviser to the Museum, who was responsible for the measures which succeeded in preserving the more fragile objects. Their continued preservation is in the care of the Department of Antiquities of the Egyptian Government.

There were also the distinguished American experts such as Lythgoe, Burton, Winlock and Mace. Dr. Derry, Sir Alan Gardiner, and Professor Percy Newberry who gave his services as

A statuette of Tutankhamen as a boy

A funerary bouquet

botanist and identified the wreaths and other floral tributes found in the tomb.

Of these men, three were known personally to me, and as death removes, one by one, the little band who first entered the tomb, it is something to have spoken to a few and heard their story first-hand.

I remember Mrs. Newberry, who died shortly after her husband, telling me about the wonderful linen pall which was found draped over the inner shrine. The most remarkable thing about it, she said, was that the hemming and stitching had been done in exactly the same way it would have been done today. It was Mrs. Newberry who carefully rethreaded the delicate jewelled necklaces now on view at the Museum in Cairo. The original thread had of course perished. After Carter had had the beads photographed exactly as they lay, Mrs. Newberry rethreaded them. 'Some of the beads,' she remarked, 'were so tiny that it would have been impossible to see the holes but for the wonderful Egyptian sunlight.'

Newberry himself told me that one of the floral wreaths, placed near the sealed door of the sepulchre, could, perhaps, have been laid there by Queen Ankhesenamun herself.

When you go to Cairo today, and enter the Museum, you may at first be slightly disappointed. The gold, after more than forty years, has a slightly tarnished appearance, as mentioned earlier. One is likely to be hustled through the Museum by dragomans (guides) along with many other tourists, and it is not always easy to recapture in one's imagination that awesome moment when Carter peered through a hole in the outer, sealed door and, with eyes growing accustomed to the light, saw everywhere the gleam of gold. . . .

Of all the human beings who have lived during the last troubled half-century, the one I envy most is Carter, the first human being to see the full glory of a Pharaoh's treasure after it had lain in darkness for over thirty centuries.

68

Part of the innermost treasury

10 Why did it Happen?

Amun-Re, King of Gods

One important question remains to be answered. Why was it that, alone among more than thirty Pharaonic tombs in the Royal Valley, that of Tutankhamen survived down to the twentieth century? Much of the credit is obviously due to the patience and persistence of Howard Carter who, even when his patron was on the point of giving up excavating in the Valley, persuaded him to finance one more season's digging, on the ground that there was one small triangular area, near the tomb of Ramesses VI, which had not been thoroughly investigated.

But there is more to it than that. All the other tombs of kings had been looted in remote antiquity. Why had that of Tutankhamen been spared, or overlooked? One could answer that it was a very small sepulchre compared with those of such mighty kings as Seti I and Ramesses II. But practically all the tombs of the nobles or high officials, situated on the eastern side of the Theban cliffs, had been systematically robbed thousands of years ago, and they were usually even smaller than that of Tutankhamen.

No, there must be some other explanation, or maybe several explanations. In my opinion the clue lies in the fact that Tutankhamen was a near relative of the so-called Heretic King Amenophis IV, who renamed himself Akhenaten which means, 'It is well with the Aten'. The 'Aten' was Akhenaten's god, a solar disk with descending rays which he intended should replace all the many deities of Egypt as the One God all men should worship. In particular he detested Amun-Re, King of Gods, whose worship was centred at Thebes and for this

70

reason the idealistic Pharaoh removed his capital to a virgin site midway between Thebes and modern Cairo. There you may still see the ruins of his short-lived city called Tell el Amarna, and the tombs of his great officials cut out of the rocky cliffs to the east. In all of these you see the symbol of the One God, the 'Aten' just as you see it on the backrest of Tutankhamen's throne.

Akhenaten's queen was the lovely Nefertiti, whose famous portrait bust, found by German excavators at Tell el Amarna, is perhaps the best-known of all Egyptian sculptured heads. Tutankhamen, originally called Tutankh*aten*, may have been her son, or at least the son of her husband by one of his other wives (for in Ancient Egypt it was permissible for a King to have several wives, besides concubines). Certainly he was brought up by her in his early youth, and there can be little doubt that some of the furniture found in his tomb came originally from the Royal Palace of Akhenaten, where Tutankhamen's girl-queen, Ankhesenamun, was also educated in the Aten-faith. Her name was originally Ankhesenpaaten.

When Akhenaten died, the Court moved back to Thebes; in fact it seems possible that toward the end of his reign Akhenaten was seeking a compromise with the priests of the older god Amun, at Thebes, and sent one of his sons, Smenkhkare, there, later to be joined by Tutankhaten (as he was still named) and his wife. One theory is that it was Nefertiti and not Akhenaten who was the most devoted 'Atenist' and that she nurtured Tutankhaten while her husband lavished his affection on Smenkhkare, who was either Tutankhaten's brother or half-brother.

The whole period is obscure; no one can be certain what happened during the declining years of the Eighteenth Dynasty (1400-1350 B.C.). The general impression is of royal children being used in a political power game between ambitious politicians such as General Horemheb and an elder stateman named Ay (or Eye). Both subsequently became Pharaohs in the

Akhenaten, father of Tutankhamen

71

Nefertiti, wife of Akhenaten, who may have been Tutankhamen's mother

usual way, by marrying the royal heiresses. This was the way power passed from a Pharaoh to his successor. To become a Pharaoh you usually married the widow or daughter of your predecessor. It was probably for this reason that brothers married sisters (or half-sisters), so that the power of succession should remain within the royal family.

What we do know for certain is that the young Tutankhaten changed his name to Tutankh-*amen*, and Ankhesenpaaten to Ankhesen*amun*, each incorporating into his or her name that of the old god Thebes, Amun. Thus Amun triumphed, and after the death of the hated heretic Akhenaten the old religion was re-established at Thebes. The Heretic King was vilified; his name was erased from his monuments and his capital destroyed.

Now imagine the situation of the young Tutankhamen and his wife at such a period. They were little more than children, given due reverence as king and queen, yet knowing all the time that they were surrounded by ambitious, scheming older people, anxious to obtain power by any means. Despite the fact that they had, officially, abandoned the New Religion and embraced the older faith, they still were members of an unpopular Dynasty. Moreover, as we know Akhenaten suffered from a disease which caused malformation of the skull and limbs, it is more than likely that Tutankhamen also was in poor health. Generations of inbreeding, brother-and-sister marriages, had weakened the royal stock. It was very near its end.

Funerary furniture was made during their brief young lives to accompany the royal bodies on the journey to the world beyond the grave. Such furniture—gilded shrines, coffins, couches, caskets, etc.—was kept in the storerooms of Amun for eventual use. But it is a curious fact that, among the objects found in the tomb of Tutankhamen there were some (e.g., the shrines) which had originally been meant for his half-brother (or brother) Smenkhkare. One can see where the royal cartouche (the name of the

Pharaoh surrounded by a flattened oval) has been altered.

Smenkhkare, who preceded Tutankhamen as Pharaoh, reigned for only a few years, and some authorities believe that the body of the young man found in the so-called 'Tomb of Tiye' (Akhenaten's mother) is that of the young Pharaoh. Others have recently advanced the theory that the body is that of the Heretic King, Akhenaten himself, pointing out that the disease from which he suffered would have had the effect of preventing the bones from attaining their normal growth, so that, though the body appears to be that of a young man it could be that of a man of forty. Again, we do not know. It is a mystery.

But to return to the tomb of Tutankhamen and the reason why it remained intact for three thousand years. Everything points to the fact that the tomb was *not* originally intended for a Pharaoh. First, it is very small compared with those of such kings as Tuthmosis III, Amenophis II, Ramesses II and Seti I. It could, possibly, have been intended for the burial of a privileged nobleman, perhaps related to the Royal Family, a man who was permitted the rare honour of being buried in the Royal Valley. The tomb of Yuya and Thuya, discovered by Theodore Davis in 1903, springs to mind.

Now the principal celebrant depicted on the wall paintings in Tutankhamen's burial chamber is the politician Ay (or Eye) who had been one of Akhenaten's closest advisers (he had another tomb prepared at Tell el Amarna) and who subsequently married Tutankhamen's widow, Ankhesenamun, and thus made himself Pharaoh. It is tempting to think that this little, insignificant sepulchre was built for Ay, and that when he became Pharaoh, on the death of Tutankhamen, he buried the boy king in the small tomb he had made for himself, while he prepared a much larger tomb to contain his own body when he died. His own tomb exists, not far from that of Amenophis III in the Western Valley, though it is not normally accessible to the public.

One of Tutankhamen's war chariots now in the Cairo Museum

73

The entrance of the innermost treasury

This would explain why the relatively minor tomb of Tutankhamen was stuffed with treasure obviously designed for a much larger burial place (remember that the outermost of the four golden shrines within the burial chamber almost touched the walls and ceiling). The Antechamber and Annex were crowded to the ceiling with marvels, and the royal chariots had had to be sawn in pieces to admit them to the narrow chamber. One may well imagine the rich Ancient Egyptian curses of the workmen who, by royal decree, were forced to assemble three royal coffins, a sarcophagus, and four wooden shrines within less than half the space which they had been intended to occupy. No wonder they put the shrines in the wrong way round, as Carter discovered!

There is no written record of this. We can only deduce the probable facts from the material evidence, like a detective following up clues. Then what happened? Clearly the position of the tomb was well known to the ancient tomb robbers, who, as we have seen, entered it more than once, but were unable to steal more than a few easily portable objects. Evidently they entered the burial chamber—the hole at the bottom of the sealed doorway proves that—but again were able only to take away a few small things. The Pharaoh's burial remained inviolate.

Clearly the guardians of the royal cemetery were, at this time, exceptionally vigilant, since they were able to prevent the thieves removing more than a few articles, and at one stage interrupted a robbery, so that one of the plunderers was forced to leave on the floor the few golden rings he had hurriedly knotted in a piece of linen, unless the thief was caught red-handed and the loot subsequently returned to the tomb.

Before resealing the entrance for what proved to be the last time for three thousand years, the priests of the Necropolis hurriedly 'tidied up' the tomb, but did not bother to restore the objects to their original caskets or boxes. Hence the scene of confusion which greeted Carter and Carnarvon when they first entered the sepulchre; hence the chaotic state of the Annex, glimpsed

75

A baked-clay tablet with cuneiform writing

through a tomb-robber's hole in the wall, wherein lay all kinds of precious things hurled higgledy-piggledy where the thieves had left them, even to the footprint of one of the would-be robbers clearly showing on a bow case.

But what happened to the girl-queen, Ankhesenamun? No one knows, except that, in the end, she married Ay, a man in his sixties. There is, however, a fascinating piece of correspondence which was found preserved in the archives of the royal capital of the Hittites at Hattusas (Boghaz-koy) in modern Turkey. The Hittites were a powerful people, ruled by kings reigning from the highlands of Asia Minor. From time to time they came into conflict with the Ancient Egyptians in Syria; the Egyptians, on their monuments, described these enemies as 'the abominable Kheta' (Hatti or Hittites) though in later years the two empires became allies.

Some sixty-odd years ago a German archaeologist named Winckler excavated Hattusas and found a large number of baked-clay tablets inscribed in the ancient Babylonian cuneiform (wedge-shaped) writing. Among these royal archives was a series of letters from an unknown Egyptian queen addressed to the Hittite King Suppiluliuma, who is known to have led his armies to the borders of Egypt's Syrian colonies round about the time of Tutankhamen's reign. The dates are not precise, but near enough.

Among these tablets (having no paper the Hittites used baked clay for their correspondence) are letters addressed to Suppiluliuma. The first reads: 'My husband has died and I have no son, but of you it is said that you have many sons. If you would send one of your sons, he could become my husband. I will on no account take one of my subjects and make him my husband. I am very much afraid. . . .'

'I am very much afraid.' This does not sound like a letter from a mature, experienced stateswoman, but from a frightened young girl.

Still, we do not know who the unknown queen was as one cannot be certain of the

76

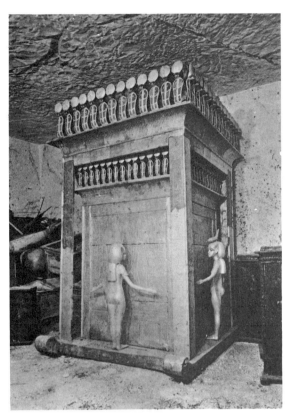

Interior of the innermost treasury

precise dates. A later letter, found in the same collection at Hattusas, is evidently written in reply to one from King Suppiluliuma which has been lost. From its content one assumes that the cautious Hittite monarch had doubted the truth of the Egyptian queen's earlier message. She replies, in some anger: 'Why do you say, "They are deceiving me?" If I had a son, would I write to a foreigner [observe the note of contempt] to publish my distress and that of my country? You have insulted me by speaking thus. . . . My husband is dead and I have no son. I will never take one of my subjects and marry him. I have written to no one but you. Everyone says you have many sons; give me one of them that he may become my husband.'

Good archaeologists like Carter are cautious people. They deal, not with written documents of known date, as historians do, but with tangible objects which can sometimes be dated. Occasionally written records turn up, as in this case, but again it is necessary to be careful in ascribing them to any particular person unless they are signed. In another letter from these Hittite archives the name of the dead Egyptian king is rendered as 'Dakhamun' which *could* be Tutankhamen. However, it is permissible to speculate and form deductions, as a good detective does, and every known fact points to the unknown queen being Ankhesenamun, Tutankhamen's widow, who was probably only sixteen when those letters were written.

Why can we assume this to be true? First, because the dates fit. Second, because we know for certain that royal inheritance in Ancient Egypt was *always through the female line*. Whoever married the heiress of a Pharaoh, whether his widow or daughter (if the wife was dead) could become Pharaoh and rule Egypt. Third, we know from the presence of the still-born children in Tutankhamen's tomb that his girl-wife had attempted to bear him children but they had died. If any of her children by Tutankhamen had survived there would almost certainly have been some record of them. Fourth, we know that Ay, who had held high rank under Akhenaten, subsequently married Ankhesenamun and became Pharaoh. These facts are on record.

What we do *not* know is what happened during the period of about one hundred days during which the Pharaoh's dead body was soaking in its bath of natron (a preservative fluid) and preparations were being made for its burial. Ay was over sixty; Ankhesenamun was probably not more than sixteen or seventeen. Would she wish to marry Ay? It seems highly unlikely. But, surrounded as she was by suave courtiers and ambitious, smooth-tongued statesmen, and knowing, as she must have, that during the brief period before her dead husband was buried no one could *compel* her to marry, what would be more natural than that she should stretch out her hand in desperation to the Hittite King, who, as she wrote (if it was

78

Ankhesenamun who wrote those letters) 'had many sons'?

It was her last chance. She was very young, probably beautiful, and, as she admits in one of her letters 'very much afraid.' My own belief is that if, indeed, Ankhesenamun wrote those pathetic letters, in which royal pride mingles with pleading, she was one of the bravest women of history. To get those letters to the Hittite King at all, without detection, was an act of great diplomatic subtlety and skill. Again, she had to risk the snubs she might (and indeed did) receive. But when she writes, defiantly 'I will on no account take one of my subjects and make him my husband' I am certain that she is thinking only of one 'subject', the ambitious, sixty-year-old politician Ay.

Alas, her gamble failed. Whether or not the Hittite King sent one of his sons, we know that in the end Tutankhamen was ceremonially buried; Ay performed the funerary rites, wearing the sacred leopard skin, as you may see him on the walls of the tomb, and subsequently he married Ankhesenamun. We hear no more of Tutankhamen's widow.

Soon a new, vigorous dynasty, the Nineteenth (1350–1200 B.C.) took the place of the old. The Pharaohs of this period, men such as Seti I, Ramesses II, and others, were warriors who, in part, regained the empire which had almost been lost by Akhenaten and his short-lived successors. It is possible that at this time, when the very name of the Heretic Pharaoh was obliterated from his monuments, that his descendants also fell into disfavour. Perhaps even the records of their burials were destroyed; we do not know.

Several attempts were made to rob Tutankhamen's tomb; we have clear evidence of that. But such attempts must have been made within a few years of the burial, when the site of the tomb was known. Why was knowledge of its position forgotten after a time? Probably because the official records of these unpopular rulers, heirs and successors of Akhenaten, were deliberately expunged. After that it was a matter

One of the king's bows

79

The large entrance to the tomb of Ramesses VI and below it the modest entrance to the tomb of Tutankhamen

of luck. Several generations later, during the Twentieth Dynasty (1200–1090 B.C.) the enormous and elaborate tomb of Ramesses VI was cut out of the hillside immediately above the tomb of Tutankhamen. The stone chippings of the excavators poured down the valley slopes and effectively concealed the entrance to the modest sepulchre of this now-forgotten Pharaoh. And so, for three thousand years, it remained concealed, until one day, at a country house in England, Carter drew his patron's attention to a triangular area on the map and said, 'We *must* dig here'.